Praise for
Finding Your Way Back to God

"The Ferguson brothers are the real deal as movement leaders, and they have led a burgeoning church-planting network on the very principle outlined in this book. As such, it is a proven guide to aligning your community with the redemptive purposes of God."

—ALAN HIRSCH, author and activist

"Even if you've never set foot in a church, you've probably heard someone say something like, 'We're all searching for God.' But that search is not a one-way street. In their new book, my friends Dave and Jon believe that more than anything else, God wants us to find him. You need to read this book and rediscover the God who's been searching for you all along."

—GREG SURRATT, founding pastor, Seacoast Church

"Dave and Jon Ferguson are passionate about helping people find their way back to God. If you know someone who is far from God or you've begun to feel that way yourself, this book is for you. Take their thirty-day challenge and awaken to the journey of a lifetime."

—LARRY OSBORNE, author and pastor, North Coast Church

"Sometimes we convince ourselves that people are hard to reach. We console our lack of spiritual fruit to a cultural malaise of all things spiritual. Dave and Jon Ferguson have another idea. They have somehow managed the incredible challenge to connect the dots of spiritual awakening in the culture and hearts of everyday people. Like expert craftsmen, they have made what is incredibly hard into real life possibilities and strategies that seem easy! I've read *Finding*

Your Way Back to God and have already considered buying a box so I can give it to all my friends and neighbors. You should too."

—DANIELLE STRICKLAND, speaker, activist, author of *A Beautiful*
Mess: How God Re-creates Our Lives

"This book is your invitation to start—or restart—your journey toward an authentic connection with God. The awakenings Dave and Jon Ferguson guide you through are nothing less than life changing. Don't miss this book!"

—MARK BATTERSON, author of *The Circle Maker*

"Ferguson presents this complex issue in a clear, straightforward manner. I am going to give this book to people I love who want to find their way back to God."

—PASTOR JOBY MARTIN, The Church of Eleven22

"Dave and Jon Ferguson provide a practical road map for any of us—whether we are distant, disillusioned, or far from God—to return to Him. This timely book is full of stories, personal reflection, and inspiring thoughts, and makes the road to be traveled and the journey to be taken both doable and enjoyable. I highly recommend it!"

—BRAD LOMENICK, author of *The Catalyst Leader* and *H3*
Leadership, past president of Catalyst, founder of BLINC

"All of us have a void in our lives that only God can fill. We need the forgiveness, hope, and purpose that only God can provide. Dave and Jon's book points us back to the great promise that addresses this eternal pursuit—if we seek God, we will find him. Embrace the journey."

—TONY MORGAN, founder and Chief Strategic Officer of The
Unstuck Group

"One of the most helpful books I've seen in a long time, *Finding Your Way Back to God* is a practical and hopeful pathway for everyone seeking a close relationship with God."

—LOUIE GIGLIO, Passion City Church/Passion Conferences

"My friends Dave and Jon have spent years focused on one compelling message: helping people find their way back to God. This book is full of inspiring stories, practical steps, and spiritual challenges to help anyone struggling with the journey. If you or someone you know is at a spiritual crossroad, I highly recommend *Finding Your Way Back to God*."

—MARK JOBE, lead pastor of New Life Community Church;
author of *Unstuck: Out of Your Cave into Your Call*

"I cannot imagine a better book for anyone who wants to find their way back to God or help others do so. It is full of inspiring stories that connect to the longings we all have. And the simple prayers and thought-provoking questions Dave and Jon suggest will change the way you look at yourself, God, and the purpose of your life."

—DR. RICK RICHARDSON, professor of Evangelism and Leadership at Wheaton College and the Billy Graham Center; author of *Experiencing Healing Prayer* and *Reimagining Evangelism*

"In their new book, Dave Ferguson and Jon Ferguson have tapped into principles that ring true all across the world. From the US to India, this book can guide people on the Jesus mission no matter what country they may call home. If you are serious about helping people find their way back to God, or if you're on the journey yourself, this is a must read! It can literally change the course of the rest of your life."

—DR. AJAI LALL, director of Central India Christian Mission

"There is a constant gap in our lives between where we are and where we want to be. For years, I've longed to have a map to help me close that gap. This book is an answer to that longing! It's a spiritual GPS to help you find where you are and to help you get where you're going. It can help you find your way back to God over and over and over again. This book isn't just for people seeking God for the first time—it's also for anyone who wants to continue to get closer to God year after year. If you took the classic *The Pilgrim's Progress,* boiled it down into the main principles, and added modern-day stories, you would have this book in your hands. It's that good!"

—JOSH HOWARD, director of Leadership Training, Central India
Christian Mission, and NewThing Network Leader

"Dave and Jon are treasure to Jesus's Church. In *Finding Your Way Back to God,* you will discover why. Likewise, trusted friends, you will be awakened to the five Awakenings of your new life in Christ. You will be encouraged."

—DERWIN L. GRAY, lead pastor of Transformation Church; author
of *The High Definition Leader*

"I can't think of a better journey to take than one that reconnects you with God and helps you to discover your purpose in life. Dave and Jon Ferguson lead you step by step in this awakening process, which will change your life."

—JAMES T. MEEKS, senior pastor of Salem Baptist Church of
Chicago; retired Illinois State Senator

FINDING
YOUR
WAY BACK
TO GOD

FINDING YOUR WAY BACK TO GOD

5 Awakenings
to Your New Life

DAVE FERGUSON & JON FERGUSON

MULTNOMAH
BOOKS

FINDING YOUR WAY BACK TO GOD
PUBLISHED BY MULTNOMAH BOOKS
12265 Oracle Boulevard, Suite 200
Colorado Springs, Colorado 80921

Scripture quotations are taken from the Holy Bible, New International Version®. NIV®. Copyright © 1973, 1978, 1984, 2011 by Biblica Inc.® Used by permission. All rights reserved worldwide. Scripture quotations marked (MSG) are taken from The Message by Eugene H. Peterson. Copyright © 1993, 1994, 1995, 1996, 2000, 2001, 2002. Used by permission of Tyndale House Publishers, Inc. All rights reserved. Scripture quotations marked (NASB) are taken from the New American Standard Bible®. © Copyright The Lockman Foundation 1960, 1962, 1963, 1968, 1971, 1972, 1973, 1975, 1977, 1995. Used by permission. (www. Lockman.org). Scripture quotations marked (NIrv) are taken from the Holy Bible, New International Reader's Version®. NIrv®. Copyright © 1995, 1996, 1998 by Biblica Inc.™ Used by permission of Zondervan. All rights reserved worldwide. www.zondervan.com. Scripture quotations marked (NLT) are taken from the Holy Bible, New Living Translation, copyright © 1996, 2004, 2007. Used by permission of Tyndale House Publishers Inc., Carol Stream, Illinois 60188. All rights reserved.

Details in some anecdotes and stories have been changed to protect the identities of the persons involved.

Excerpt from *The Ragamuffin Gospel: Good News for the Bedraggled, Beat-Up, and Burnt Out* by Brennan Manning, copyright © 1990 by Brennan Manning. Used by permission of WaterBrook Multnomah, an imprint of the Crown Publishing Group, a division of Penguin Random House LLC. All rights reserved.

Trade Paperback ISBN 978-1-60142-609-3
Hardcover ISBN 978-1-60142-608-6
eBook ISBN 978-1-60142-610-9

Cover design by Mark D. Ford

Published in the United States by WaterBrook Multnomah, an imprint of the Crown Publishing Group, a division of Penguin Random House LLC, New York.

MULTNOMAH® and its mountain colophon are registered trademarks of Penguin Random House LLC.

The Library of Congress has cataloged the hardcover edition as follows:
Ferguson, Dave, 1962–
  Finding your way back to God : 5 awakenings to your new life / Dave Ferguson & Jon Ferguson.
—First Edition.
      pages cm
    ISBN 978-1-60142-608-6—ISBN 978-1-60142-610-9 (electronic) 1. Christian life. 2. Religious awakening—Christianity. I. Title.
    BV4509.5.F443 2015
    248.4—dc23

                        2014040979

Printed in the United States of America
2016

10 9 8 7 6 5 4 3

SPECIAL SALES
Most WaterBrook Multnomah books are available at special quantity discounts when purchased in bulk by corporations, organizations, and special-interest groups. Custom imprinting or excerpting can also be done to fit special needs. For information, please e-mail SpecialMarkets@WaterBrookMultnomah.com or call 1-800-603-7051.

This book is dedicated
to the inspiring people of
COMMUNITY
and their relentless passion for hpftwbtG!

CONTENTS

AWAKENING TO LIFE: "Now this is living!"

The Journey Starts Here

You can find your way back to God.

You're invited to go on a journey, one that could change your life in big and significant ways. This journey, like every other, is ultimately about closing the distance between where you are now and where you want to be.

Finding Your Way Back to God is a map for every traveler on this journey. All of us feel lost on this road at some point in our lives — sometimes really lost, and sometimes for a really long time. Whatever "God talk" people use to describe the experience of this journey, most would agree it comes down to a simple yet overwhelming longing: *We want to find our way home.*

We want to feel personally connected to the One who made us, who knows us for who we are. Who might even be able to help us. We feel powerfully drawn to move toward God, even when we fumble for words to explain it. Or him.

Does any of this ring true for you?

This book is based on a principle that may surprise you. *Not only is the longing to find God a universal experience, but there is also a universal pattern for what a journey in his direction looks like:*

- What twists and turns, what long, dark stretches you can expect.
- What mile markers—in this book we call them *awakenings*—to watch for.
- What home actually looks like, so you'll know it when you get there.

The best account of this finding-your-way-back-to-God experience comes in a story. We'll show it to you. It's a story Jesus told about a young man who set out to find the good life, only to end up lost and lonely. You don't have to know much about Jesus today to make the wisdom of his story work for you.

And here's one more principle: *God wants to be found even more than you want to find him.*

Now, if you've been distant from God for years, you're not likely to believe that. Not for a minute.

But we do. Based on our experience with thousands of travelers much like you, and based even more on the story Jesus told, we believe that God wants to be found. We believe, actually, that before you make your first move in his direction, he's already moving in yours.

We believe this so much that we're willing to put it to a test. We call it the 30-Day Wager. You take the risk to begin each day with a prayer. You ask God to show up. Then see if he responds.

Do you dare?

1

When Did You Forget About God?

Nick is a big, tough, blue-collar guy who grew up in an equally tough neighborhood of Chicago.

A few months before he was born, his dad left the family for another woman who had her own little boy. Nick told me, "I can remember growing up in a nasty, bug-infested apartment with my mom and two older brothers. Meanwhile, on the other side of town, my biological father, his new wife, and his stepson lived in a nice house with no bugs. I remember asking, 'God, if you are so good, why would you let this happen to a little kid like me?'"

Nick's confusion turned to doubt, his doubt evolved into indifference, and then his indifference turned into amnesia. Nick forgot about God and moved on.

Several years later, when Lisa came into Nick's life, she brought a spiritual curiosity that Nick had long lost. She was the best thing that had ever happened to him. As Lisa began her own search for God, Nick saw her changing for the better. She was more patient, worried less, and was clearly full of life.

Nick wanted some of that and decided to give God one more chance. Without telling anyone, he secretly started praying, "God, if you are real, make yourself real to me." He said that prayer every day, and he noticed

3

changes in his life. He felt more at peace, more hopeful. He found that he was having conversations about God and meeting people who believed in God. Occurrences took place that he called "God things." It seemed that God might be answering his prayer, but he was still waiting to be sure.

Nick was like many people who are trying their best to find their way back to God.

Maybe he's a little like you.

A FINDABLE GOD

The fact that you are reading this book suggests to me that you or someone close to you has an interest in spiritual matters. You may feel distant from God yet not sure how to close the gap. You might be reaching out to God for the first time, or you might be reaching out again.

I—Dave—know what that is like. So does my brother, Jon. We have both made and continue to make our own journeys back to God. And we are writing this book equally and together (even though for convenience, we'll mostly be writing as "I").

I have personally seen God's faithfulness as I seek him, not once but over and over again, and not just a long time ago but recently. Here's how it works. I find myself far from God. Then, like a little kid who is lost, I cry out, and my heavenly Father always responds, "Here I am."

When I was in grade school and afraid of dying, he was there.

When I was a teen and never felt good enough, he was there.

When I was a young adult, feeling beat up by doubts and failures, he was there.

When I have made choices that are opposite to what I say I value, he has been there.

When I have been alone and needed guidance, he has been there.

When I feel like giving up, he is there.

Sure, there have been times when I haven't *felt* like he was there. But I always realized, eventually, that he actually *was* there. The whole time.

For more than twenty years, I have been a pastor of a church, and I have seen thousands of people from every walk of life travel the journey that I have taken and that I am about to take you on. It's been such a privilege. And it has cemented my conviction that God is a God who wants to be found and welcomes all who return to him.

I'll be telling the stories of many of these people throughout the book. This is not to entertain you but to give you pictures of what it looks like to return to God. The stories and testimonies of those who have gone before us on this journey outline a well-worn path across an open field. Each adventure is personal, but we can see the path ahead because of others who have traveled before us.

I'm not saying it's always easy. But it's so worth it. The journey back to God promises freedom, grace, and forgiveness for everything in our pasts. We can find meaning and redemption, even in the darkest parts of our stories.

Does that sound appealing to you? If so, then let me ask you a question: How did you forget God?

SPIRITUAL AMNESIA

If I were to give you a survey with the question, Do you believe in God? with boxes where you would check "yes" or "no," most likely you would check the box for "yes." According to a Gallup survey, 92 percent of Americans would check "yes."[1] So the great majority of us do believe in the existence of God.

The problem is that we forget him.

You may have heard the story told by author Dan Millman of a little girl named Sachi and her unforgettable request.

Soon after her brother was born, little Sachi began to ask her parents to leave her alone with the new baby. They worried that, like most four-year-olds, she might feel jealous and want to hit or shake him, so they said no. But she showed no signs of jealousy and she treated the baby with kindness—and her pleas to be left alone with him became more urgent. They decided to allow it.

Elated, she went into the baby's room and shut the door, but it opened a crack—enough for her curious parents to peek in and listen. They saw little Sachi walk quietly up to her baby brother, put her face close to his, and say quietly, "Baby, tell me what God is like. I'm starting to forget."[2]

For many of us, there is a point in time we can look back on and say, "That is when I forgot about God." Others of us would say, "That's when it felt like God forgot about me."

For you, that point in time might have been in your childhood, when God should have been there and he wasn't. Behind closed doors you were left vulnerable to the kind of treatment no child should ever endure. It felt as if God were locked out of your house and couldn't get in.

Or maybe you remember the day the fighting escalated. Your dad was yelling and your mom was crying; then the door slammed and your father left. You didn't see God leave, but as a kid, it felt like that was the moment he walked out too.

Maybe it was during your growing-up years that you forgot about God. When you most needed to be accepted and included, you were left all alone and on the outside looking in. It made sense even then that, if there were a God, he wouldn't have abandoned you.

Or there was a loss or a death that you know God could have prevented, but for reasons you still don't understand, he did not.

Perhaps right now it feels to you as if God has forgotten about you. Something has gone terribly wrong in your life. You have prayed and prayed and prayed—and nothing has changed.

Or you've done something wrong, and you know you have put distance between yourself and God. But you don't know how to bridge that gulf.

Or you have objections to doctrines, intellectual doubts you have no answers for, or disappointments about religious people that put you off. Maybe these are obstacles you can never get over.

So often you sit in that sacred space, waiting, anticipating, sometimes praying, but nothing changes. You keep showing up for the religious service, but it seems like God never does.

Whatever your reason for feeling distant from God, it's possible for you to start the journey back to him.

"GOD, IF . . ."

Kelly would tell you that she gave up on God when she was fifteen. Her mom pushed her to go to church, forced her to go through confirmation, and made her go to her first communion. In spite of her mother's good intentions, none of it made sense to Kelly. By the time she was fifteen, she says, she'd had enough.

I know Kelly, and I think she actually forgot about God long before she turned fifteen. If you could visit her Facebook page, you would see that the cover photo shows Kelly holding her two-year-old son while sitting in a grave-yard in front of her father's tombstone. Kelly's dad died when she was only four months old. Kelly told me, "I think, in some ways, I didn't want to believe in God—my dad died, my brothers didn't really look out for me, and my boyfriend was abusive. It was hard to believe there was a good guy out there. And since God was supposed to be a 'Father,' I didn't want to let him in."

So she started forgetting about God, and by the time she was fifteen, she said, "God was far, far, far away."

When I first met Kelly, she had just graduated from high school, where she had been a cheerleader, was on the dean's list, and had lots of friends and a life full of promise. Kelly decided not to go to college and started waiting tables at a breakfast restaurant I frequent. At the time she didn't know me as the pastor of a church. I was just a guy named Dave who happened to sit in her section on Wednesdays.

Over the next several years, Kelly dated several men who gave her nothing, with the exception of a beautiful baby boy. Her youthful exuberance, her hopes and dreams gradually all wore away. Through it all, her constant friend was a bottle.

Then one day I went to see her in the hospital; she looked like death. She had drunk herself into a coma—whether by accident or in a deliberate attempt to kill herself, I didn't know. Although she was conscious by the time I visited her, the staff at the hospital still weren't sure she'd make it. I wondered if I would ever see her again.

A few months later, I got a text and then a call from Kelly. She told me she always felt comfortable talking to me about spiritual matters and wanted to know if we could meet. So we met at Starbucks the next Thursday. She told me that she had been sober for a few weeks and was working the Twelve Steps of Alcoholics Anonymous. Then she looked at me with a deep sincerity and said, "Dave, can you help me believe in God?"

I said I would try my best, and we agreed to meet the following Thursday. It was the first in a long series of weekly conversations. The second week I bought coffee and showed her a Bible verse that was meaningful to me. In it God promises, "You will seek me and find me when you seek me with all your heart."[3] Then I advised her, "Every day, ask God to deliver on this promise. Just say to him, 'God, if you are real, make yourself real to me.' And let's see what happens."

She looked at me as if she wanted to trust me on this but didn't know if she could.

I'll tell you the outcome of Kelly's story before this chapter is done. But first let me point something out. Kelly was a lot like Nick, and she was a lot like many of us, in one sense: if she ever understood her identity as God's child, she had forgotten it.

It's strange how people are capable of forgetting who they are.

"I KNOW WHO YOU ARE"

For Ed Smart it was worse than a nightmare when he faced a horde of reporters and television journalists who had camped out on his front lawn. Overcome with emotion, this father stepped up to the battery of microphones and spoke directly to his daughter. "Elizabeth," he said, "if you are out there, we are doing everything we possibly can to help you." He fought back the tears and then addressed the kidnappers, "Please let her go. Please!" People all over the country felt anxiety for the Smarts and their fourteen-year-old Elizabeth, who had been abducted from her bedroom the night before.

For the next nine months, her kidnappers held Elizabeth captive. Forced to wear a wig and a disguise, she would often be close to her Salt Lake City home, but no one ever recognized her. On occasion, she and her abductors would eat at restaurants her family frequented, but no one identified her. Experts believe it's possible that, as sometimes happens in an abduction, Stockholm syndrome began to set in. Elizabeth no longer identified with the Smarts as her family and their home as her true home. Instead, she began to sympathize and identify with her oppressors.

Nine months later, Elizabeth Smart was at a crossroads, literally and figuratively.

A police officer spotted a vaguely familiar teenage girl crossing an intersection in Sandy, Utah. After the policeman asked a few questions, the teenage girl blurted out, "I know you think I'm Elizabeth Smart, but I'm not."[4] The police officer asked about the wig she was wearing. She insisted that it was her real hair. The officer questioned her about the couple she was with, and she was adamant that they were her parents, even though they were in fact her kidnappers.

So lost, but so close to home.

So close to being found, but not even knowing it.

Apparently, the painful events of the past months had been too much for her. She had either repressed the memories of the rapes, captivity, and indoctrination she had been through or simply couldn't deal with them. It was as though she didn't even know she was lost anymore. She had forgotten who she really was and to whom she belonged. It almost kept her from being found and going home.

But then the officer looked her in the eye and gently said something along these lines: "I know who you are. You are Elizabeth Smart. You've been lost. And I'd like to take you home."

Silence.

He showed her a missing-person poster featuring a photograph of herself.

Then she looked up with tears brimming in her eyes and said, "Thou sayeth, I'll say it."[5] In other words, "If you say so."

YOUR LIFE AT THE CROSSROADS

I believe God has you reading this book right now because he wants you to hear him gently speak to you, "I know who you are. And I know that your journey has taken you to places where I never intended for you to go. Life has brought you pain I never wanted you to feel. You have experienced regret that I hoped you could have avoided. You feel lost. Now I would like to bring you home."

Sometimes it's the disappointments and tragedies of life that leave us feeling lost. We often get ourselves lost too. We make wrong turns or take detours and end up in places we never wanted to go and never thought we would be. One of the ancient prophets compares us to wayward animals, confessing,

> We all, like sheep, have gone astray,
>   each of us has turned to our own way.[6]

Some of us have been distant or lost for a long time. We've been lost for so long that we have started to identify with our own lostness.

"I'm a relational failure."

"I am a workaholic."

"I'm an addict."

Identity always precedes behavior. What you need is someone to come alongside you and help you remember who you are and to whom you belong.

You are a child of God.

You belong to God.

Remember?

For more than nine-tenths of us, believing that God exists is not the problem. The real issue is belonging. We have lost track of how to be in relationship with God. Because the truth is that, no matter who you are or what you've done or what's been done to you, you are a child, away from home, who belongs to a Father who wants to help you out of your lostness.

What the Journey Is, What It Isn't

Before we go any further, let Jon and me be as clear as we possibly can about what finding your way back to God is *not* and what it *is*.

Finding your way back to God is *not* about getting your act together or getting more religious.

Finding your way back to God is *not* about cleaning yourself up or just becoming a better person.

Finding your way back to God is *not* about eliminating all your doubts. That won't happen in this life.

Finding your way back to God is *not* about cutting a deal with God or figuring out a way to get him to accept you so that you will go to heaven when you die.

Finding your way back to God *is* for you if you want a power greater than yourself to make it through life.

Finding your way back to God *is* for you if you want to discover an unconditional love so powerful that it can transform how you think and feel every day.

Finding your way back to God *is* for people who desire a way to love others the way they need to be loved.

Finding your way back to God *is* for people who want a purpose for life that will get them out of bed, excited to meet each day.

Finding your way back to God *is* for anyone who wants a hope for this life and the next.

If that sounds good to you, let me assure you that finding your way back to God is possible. But I won't lie to you. There's no guarantee. It can go either way.

Do you remember Kelly the waitress? It was one year after almost dying of an alcohol overdose that she went back to the same hospital. But this time she went as a visitor to say thanks to the doctors and nurses who had cared for her. When she walked into the intensive care unit, one of the nurses welcomed her with a hug, saying, "Kelly, it's so good to see you."

Kelly broke down sobbing.

She recalls, "It just hit me that I was really alive, and I could have been gone. Forever. I would have missed so much. I realized that it was something more than the medicine, monitors, and doctors that kept me alive. It was God. He kept me alive because he loves me and he wants me to be there for my little boy and to help others."

I still meet with Kelly every week, and it is so good to see her taking those first steps back to God.

But tough-guy Nick's story is different from Kelly's. Despite asking God to make himself real, and despite God's showing up in ways that Nick himself described as "supernatural," he headed in the direction of home only to drift again. It can happen to any of us. I'm hoping that if Nick should ever read these words, he will keep reading and eventually find his way back. At least for now, he's still on the road.

The rest of this book is written for people like Nick, Kelly, Jon, and myself. People who find themselves, for a variety of reasons and in different seasons, having forgotten about God.

Whether you call yourself Christian, Jewish, Buddhist, Muslim, Hindu, or "none of the above," this book can help you find your way back to God. It doesn't matter if you are straight, gay, lesbian, or sexually questioning—if you want to find your way back to God, this book is for you. You can be a tight-fisted conservative or a bleeding-heart liberal or somewhere in between, and it doesn't matter—you can find your way back to God. Whether you are young or old, single, married, divorced, or widowed, there is a God out there who wants to know you, love you, and give your life purpose and meaning.

To get there, though, you're going to have to take a risk.

Maybe you're not so sure God is out there and waiting for you to come back to him. You want to bet?

2

The Wager

Conor Murphy's whole life changed with a single wager.

He was twenty-nine years old and working at a horse stable, and he wanted more out of life. Doing his job as a hired hand was like being a hotel housekeeper, except the guests were fifteen-hundred-pound horses. What he really wanted to do, instead of just cleaning up after horses, was to train and race them.

In what seemed like a crazy bet, he wagered seventy-five dollars that five of his boss's horses would win in a single day. The type of bet he made is called an "accumulator bet." If all five horses won their races, Conor would win big, but if any of the five lost, he would lose his seventy-five dollars.

All five horses crossed the finish line first that day! That single wager paid Conor Murphy $1.5 million. "Pure luck!" he called it. He put down his manure shovel, bought a house in Louisville, and pursued his dream of training horses.[7]

We love those kinds of stories. We dream of a huge win like that one being our story and a Hollywood production company making a movie about us. We know, however, that the house always has the odds in its favor, so we figure betting is a losing proposition. As we've all been warned, "If it sounds too good to be true, it probably is."

But what if there were a single wager that really would change your whole life? What if there were a way for you to win big and change everything?

BETTING ON GOD

The seventeenth-century mathematician Blaise Pascal is considered to have had one of the greatest intellects in the history of Western civilization. He grew up knowing about God, but not earnestly following him. Then, in a profound middle-of-the-night experience of God, he had a change of heart. That experience ignited Pascal's passion to help people find their way back to God.

Pascal began to challenge his fellow intellectuals to a wager on God. He would dare them to step into a belief about God and see if it didn't change their lives. Pascal explained his wager this way: "Let us weigh the gain and the loss in wagering that God is. Let us estimate these two chances. If you gain, you gain all; if you lose, you lose nothing. Wager, then, without hesitation that He is."[8]

In finding your way back to God, here is your first step: make Pascal's wager. With this gamble you have everything to gain and nothing to lose. Consider the upside. If you find God, you may also find the source of unconditional love for which you have always longed. Finding God might offer you a life-giving purpose and a genuine cause for your life. God is the One who can take your past and make sense out of it. That's a big-time payoff! And the downside? Nothing! *Nada!*

So place a bet on God. A bet is simply the decision to risk something on a possible positive outcome. The risk I want you to take is this—pray to God.

It may seem awkward at first, but I want you to try it. Talk to God and be open to the possibility that God is waiting, listening, and eager to respond.

If you will risk praying to God and inviting him into your life, the possible outcome is that God will show up. In fact, God is so passionate about having a relationship with you that I *promise* you will encounter him. Jon and I have seen it happen so many times. When you reach out to God, he responds. I'm telling you, he will. This is a bet worth making!

I have selected several prayers that I will ask you to say as a way of making the wager. Each of them will be an expansion on the first prayer. It's the same prayer that Nick and Kelly in the first chapter spoke:

> God, if you are real,
> make yourself real to me.

Every time you feel like talking to God, speak this prayer and make the wager that he's listening. I promise he is! We have his word on it.

"WHEN YOU SEEK ME . . ."

What do you think about the Bible?

You may think it's outdated or full of inconsistencies. But more likely, if you're similar to most people, you respect the Bible; maybe you even think it is one of the best sources of spiritual truth available to us. Just as the great majority of Americans believe in the existence of God, so fully three-quarters of us believe the Bible is "in some way connected to God."[9]

Throughout this sacred text, God promises that if you will seek him, you will find him. Let me show you how God makes this promise over and over again. The first promise is one you'll recognize, because it's the one I quoted to Kelly in the last chapter:

"You will call on me and come and pray to me, and I will listen to you. You will seek me and find me when you seek me with all your heart. I will be found by you," declares the LORD.[10]

Many more verses make the same promise in different ways. Here are a few:

If . . . you seek the LORD your God, you will find him if you seek him with all your heart and with all your soul.[11]

"I love those who love me;" [says the LORD,]
   "and those who diligently seek me will find me."[12]

Draw near to God and He will draw near to you.[13]

Did you hear the theme in each of those sacred verses? Over and over again, the Bible tells us that our sincere seeking results in experiencing and finding God. When we pray, "God, if you are real, make yourself real to me," he does it!

So make the bet. Wager on God. I dare you.

THIRTY DAYS TO TRY IT OUT

There's nothing magical about the wording of the "God, if you are real . . ." prayer wager. But there *is* something supernatural about the way God responds to it.

To help you not just say the words of the prayer with your mouth but also work the intent of it into your life, Jon and I are providing a 30-Day Wager guide for you at the back of this book. If you're the kind of person who likes a specific plan to grab on to, you'll be glad to use this guide. It gives you simple activities and a short—but not too short—horizon to see your wager with God pay off.

If you follow the 30-Day Wager faithfully, you will pray each of the five "God, if you are real . . ." prayers for six days at a time. In addition, you will apply the meanings of those prayers to your own life through reflection and journaling. Put your finger in the book right here, and flip to the back to check out for yourself what the 30-Day Wager looks like.

Our suggestion is this: Keep reading the book at your own pace. But however long it takes to read the book, also be working through the thirty days methodically. The 30-Day Wager may be just the tool you need to help you get started on a journey with higher stakes than even Conor Murphy gambled for—finding God!

HPFTWBTG

Jon and I have seen firsthand how thousands of people have made the wager on God and when they decided to seek him, found him. When they drew near to God, God drew near to them. In the pages to come, you will hear from people whose stories begin like this:

- Holly saw her husband disabled by depression and her family disintegrate, and she felt her whole world was collapsing.
- Jeremy and Melissa, two beautiful people, could never find love.
- Rich was a successful megachurch pastor, until his wife left, taking the kids and saying, "We can do just fine without you."
- Aaron claimed to be an atheist and had no time for God.

- Jeff's life was all about moving from one buzz to the next.
- Rick nearly lost his wife on their wedding night, due to a stroke, and kept asking, "Why?"

Each of these people, for a variety of reasons, made a bet on God, and God came through. Not all their stories have fairy-tale endings, but when they grasped for God, he embraced them. He always does.

Because of the profound and positive life changes I have experienced in my own life and have seen in these people, I have made it my life's mission to help people find their way back to God. If I were to put it on a T-shirt, it would look like this: "hpftwbtG." That is what I love to do. It is what I'm doing in this book.

5 AWAKENINGS THAT CHANGE EVERYTHING

In my observations and interactions with thousands of people, I have seen five different awakenings that almost always occur in a person's journey back to God. Where people start and what motivates them to begin this journey are often different, but the stages they go through are remarkably similar. The most common reaction I receive from people as I share these five awakenings is something like "Yeah, that's me, all right" or "How did you know?"

The five different "God, if you are real . . ." prayers are intended to arouse in you the five awakenings. They guide you in going from just feeling sad and discouraged about the distance between you and God to actually making progress in finding your way back to him.

An awakening is sort of like an *Aha!* epiphany, but it doesn't necessarily happen all of a sudden. It's often more like emerging gradually from sleep. Something enters your consciousness. You become aware that you have moved from dark to light, from old to new. Where before you didn't have an insight, now you do. And the result of it is that you have a breakthrough in understanding that enables you to get unstuck and move one giant step closer to God.

The truth behind an awakening is not something we simply comprehend, like "Paris is the capital of France" or "Cubs fans don't know when to give up." We don't just *understand* such a truth. If it is going to make a difference in our lives, we have to *realize* it—literally, see it become *real* in our own experience. It becomes a part of us.

In the rest of the book, we'll be exploring the following awakenings:

1. *An awakening to longing:* "There's got to be more."
2. *An awakening to regret:* "I wish I could start over."
3. *An awakening to help:* "I can't do this on my own."
4. *An awakening to love:* "God loves me deeply after all."
5. *An awakening to life:* "Now this is living!"

I have great confidence that these five awakenings will resonate with you, not only because I've seen them happen in many people's lives, but also because they are found in Jesus's famous story of the lost son who finds his way home. The parable of the lost son (also known as the parable of the prodigal son) is widely considered to be one of the greatest short stories in all of literature. The reason Jesus told this story is to show us how to find our way back to God. After all, that was Jesus's life mission—"to seek and to save the lost."[14]

The lost son's story is my story. It's your story. It's our story.

Even if you're already familiar with the story, please read it again. See if you can spot for yourself the turning points in the son's journey. Afterward, let's get started on the first awakening. I know the awakening to longing will tug at something deep within you.

The Story of the Lost Son

Luke 15:11–24

There was a man who had two sons. The younger one said to his father, "Father, give me my share of the estate." So he divided his property between them.

Not long after that, the younger son got together all he had, set off for a distant country and there squandered his wealth in wild living. After he had spent everything, there was a severe famine in that whole country, and he began to be in need. So he went and hired himself out to a citizen of that country, who sent him to his fields to feed pigs. He longed to fill his stomach with the pods that the pigs were eating, but no one gave him anything.

When he came to his senses, he said, "How many of my father's hired servants have food to spare, and here I am starving to death! I will set out and go back to my father and say to him: Father, I have sinned against heaven and against you. I am no longer worthy to be called your son; make me like one of your hired servants." So he got up and went to his father.

But while he was still a long way off, his father saw him and was filled with compassion for him; he ran to his son, threw his arms around him and kissed him.

The son said to him, "Father, I have sinned against heaven and against you. I am no longer worthy to be called your son."

But the father said to his servants, "Quick! Bring the best robe and put it on him. Put a ring on his finger and sandals on his feet. Bring the fattened calf and kill it. Let's have a feast and celebrate. For this son of mine was dead and is alive again; he was lost and is found." So they began to celebrate.

AWAKENING **TO** LONGING:

"There's got to be more."

The younger son . . . set off
for a distant country.
—Luke 15:13

3

"I Want What's Coming to Me"

In the movie *Scarface,* Cuban refugee Tony Montana, played by Al Pacino, becomes a drug cartel kingpin. In one scene he is cruising the streets of Miami in his convertible with his friend Manny, and they have the following exchange:

> **Manny:** I say be happy with what you got.
> **Tony:** You be happy. Me, I want what's coming to me.
> **Manny:** Oh, well what's coming to you?
> **Tony:** The world, *chico,* and everything in it![15]

Long before Tony Montana ever said, "I want what's coming to me," Jesus told a story about a young man who said essentially the same thing to his father. Jesus's famous story of the lost son starts like this: "There was a man who had two sons. The younger one said to his father, 'Father, give me my share of the estate.'"[16] In other words, "I want what's coming to me."

Jesus told the story of the lost son in the context of a first-century Middle Eastern culture. In that day, a son's asking for his inheritance early was one of the worst insults a father could receive. A son in Jesus's day was expected not only to wait until his father died to receive his inheritance but also to take care of his father in his old age. So this son asking for his inheritance early was like saying, "Look, Dad, I don't really care if you live or die anymore. I just want what's coming to me, and I want it now." This was a huge offense!

Now, before we cast this son aside as ungrateful and selfish, let's consider whether it's possible that he said out loud what most of us feel. Don't we sometimes feel that life isn't bringing us what we hoped for or what we wanted or even think we deserve?

What you're about to read next may surprise you: Thinking and feeling that you want what's coming to you is what you *should* feel. Not that everything you might desire is necessarily good for you, any more than all the things Tony Montana wanted were good. Yet your longing for a love that will truly last and a purpose for living, and your need to make sense of the hard things in life, all come from your Creator. When you awaken to the true meaning of these longings, you take a first step in your journey toward God.

So the problem isn't that we have longings or desires. The problem is that, in seeking to fulfill them on our own, we lose track of who we really are and what we were really made for.

The son in Jesus's story was like so many of us—he was convinced that he had to leave his father to fulfill his cravings and longings. So he "set off for a distant country."[17] He reminds me of my cousin Jake.

CHASING NASHVILLE

Jake grew up at a Christian summer youth camp that his parents managed, and he faithfully attended a church that his grandparents started when his mom was a teenager. His parents weren't perfect, but they nurtured and cared for him as well as anyone could imagine. When it came to spiritual direction, they seemed to strike the balance so many parents strive for—providing clear direction without being too controlling. Jake also had grandparents living nearby who filled in where his mom and dad fell short.

After high school, Jake studied music and Bible at a Christian college and soon started working part time in a local church in the suburbs of Chicago. Eventually he decided to give music his full attention, so he transitioned to downtown Chicago for a summer to work and prepare to eventually make a move to Nashville. That summer is when the drinking started.

Jake will tell you that the food and beverage industry is a good place to make quick money and foolish decisions. Both began for him while he was working at the House of Blues on North Dearborn Street. "That is where the slide to the bottom began," says Jake. "There was nothing much better on this earth than a drink after working your tail off in a bar."

When Jake made the move to Nashville, he took with him a standard operating procedure: writing music, working, chasing girls, and drinking. Jake says, "I loved to have fun and feel good. I was always joking that I was a hedonist and never fully realizing how true it was becoming."

After about five years of this routine, a subtle change took place. Jake said he no longer drank as an accompaniment to other pleasures. Instead, drinking *became* his pleasure. He told me, "I didn't drink to ease the depression or pain. Drinking was simply what I loved to do."

But alcohol was beginning to take a toll. Jake began to spiral downward into addiction. He still functioned in a relatively normal way, but he always had alcohol in his system, usually starting to drink as soon as he woke up. He got to a point where he had to drink or he would get sick. He would openly party most nights so that, when his coworkers smelled alcohol on him in the morning, they would think it was from the night before and not from the drink he'd had just before showing up for work.

It was a warm Sunday night in July when Jake knew he had to make some changes or he would not survive his lifestyle. There was no specific incident or angelic appearance to reinforce it, just a certainty that he was out of time. If he didn't stop drinking quickly, death or other serious consequences were inevitable.

"Unfortunately," he said, "I couldn't stop that Sunday night because I had to work the next three days, and I knew I wouldn't make it without drinking. So I decided I would stop on Wednesday night after work. On that Wednesday night, my body went into withdrawal, and it lasted until Saturday morning around eleven. I had something similar to a seizure every fifteen to thirty minutes, along with mild hallucinations and constant vomiting. It was terrifying, and I believed the entire time that my heart was trying to beat its way out of my rib cage.

"I prayed one prayer the whole time: 'Lord, have mercy.' It was a prayer from a book about a Celtic monk that I had read a thousand times. It was the only prayer that came to mind."

THERE'S GOT TO BE MORE

What Jake was chasing in Music City is what so many of us ultimately long for: purpose, success, love. His booze addiction was an indicator of how far he'd fallen short of finding what he really wanted. Like the son in Jesus's story, Jake had wandered off the ranch, looking for the good life in all the wrong places.

God responded to my cousin's prayer for mercy. He's been sober now for two and a half years. He'd say he's still rough around the edges, but he's totally convinced that God has a plan for the rest of his life.

If you have the feeling that you are chasing something that will never fully satisfy, pay attention to that feeling. It's from God.

Your situation might be different from Jake's. You might not be a rebel with a substance-abuse issue. In fact, I've known a lot of "good church people" who sit in a service every week—or who preach from a pulpit to those people—and who feel themselves to be far from God. They're "successful" or "put together" or "righteous" on the outside but missing God on the inside. Keeping busy with religious practices and work, school, or family just isn't enough. They need God to feel real to them as much as Jake did.

For all of us, the first awakening is a longing: "There's got to be more." This is what the lost son felt when he asked for his inheritance and left home. He didn't realize that what he longed for was already there for him.

When you long for a love that is deep and satisfying, when you want to give yourself to something that will truly make a difference, or when you seek answers to life's most difficult questions, you are trying to find your way back to God. You've really got two options: you can keep searching to fill these longings on your own, or you can look to the One who gave you those longings in the first place.

I ask that, just as Jake prayed "Lord have mercy," you will pray a particular prayer in each awakening as part of your wager that God will reveal himself to you. This is the prayer for the first awakening:

> **God, if you are real,
> make yourself real to me.
> Awaken in me the ability to see
> that you are what's missing from my life.**

My challenge for you is this: Let the meaning of that prayer sink deep into your soul. Don't let it be just words you recite. Say the prayer anticipating that God will show you he is what's missing in your life. If you are willing to make this wager, God will show you that what you are longing for can be found in him.

In the next few chapters, I want to help you discover your true inheritance: the love you long for, a purpose to give your life tremendous meaning, and answers to some of life's most difficult questions.

4

Looking for Love

Glynn Wolfe holds the record for the highest number of marriages in the United States—twenty-nine! His longest marriage lasted seven years. His shortest marriage was nineteen days. And here's an interesting detail regarding Glynn Wolfe: he was a Baptist minister.

Wolfe's son from marriage fourteen was asked why his dad got married so many times. He said, "My dad was just picky."[18]

It's easy to think, *He wasn't picky. He was pathological.* And I'm not saying he wasn't. I'm just saying that we may be a lot more like Glynn Wolfe than we care to admit. You and I are looking for love, sometimes desperately.

Why didn't Glynn Wolfe stop after his fourth or twenty-fourth attempt at wedded bliss? Why did he keep trying?

Why do most people keep trying? After all, relationships are hard. We get dumped. We get hurt. Yet we still long for love.

If you're a parent, why have another child when, no matter how wonderful they are, at some point your children break your heart? You are looking for love.

Why, if one friend stabs you in the back, do you find yourself reaching out and risking friendship again? You are looking for love.

Sometimes human relationships add incredible richness to our lives. Sometimes they just bring sorrow. But none of these relationships can fulfill the deepest longing for love in our hearts. That's why, in our journey to find God, we need to pay attention to whether our desire for love is distracting us or is leading us to him.

KNOCKING ON THE DOOR OF A BROTHEL

The son in Jesus's story took his inheritance and left home for a distant country. The story doesn't give us many details of what actually occurred in this distant country. It simply tells us,

The younger son . . . squandered his wealth in wild living.[19]

We're left to imagine what "wild living" might have looked like in Jesus's day.

If the story were told today, the son could have ventured off to Nashville or Las Vegas or Amsterdam in search of something more. I can imagine a journey that included parties with binge drinking into all hours of the night and women who were willing to satisfy every desire. His older brother tattled to his father, "This son of yours . . . has squandered your property with prostitutes."[20]

The younger brother simply pursued what we all long for, and he found this pursuit on his own to be just as empty and meaningless as we find it to be today.

I've heard it said that every man who knocks on the door of a brothel is really looking for God. If you are knocking on the door of some self-destructive behavior or relationship, you might actually have arrived at an important point in your journey back to God. Why? Because the disappointment you inevitably feel in cheap substitutes will make you wonder where you can find real love.

Our longing for real love goes all the way back to how the human race was made in the first place. God intended that we experience his love both directly from him and through others we relate to in a healthy way.

WE LONG FOR LOVE FROM OTHERS

If you listen closely to the creation account in Genesis, you hear a rhythmic repetition. After every act of creation (light, sky, dry ground, and all the rest), the story tells us, "And God saw that it was good."[21] The reviews of earth in its early state were all positive.

But then the rhythm suddenly changes. As we read that God created the first human, we find these words: "not good." And what's the reason? Loneliness. God said,

It is not good for the man to be alone.[22]

God was not just saying that the first man needed a wife. His statement went deeper than that. He was saying that our longing for love and intimacy is part of our inheritance from him. He knew from the beginning that it will feel *not good* if we are all alone. We long for loving relationships with others, and if we don't get them, our lives feel empty.

"YOU COULD FEEL THE DARKNESS"

If you were to walk past Jeremy and Melissa, you would probably notice this attractive married couple in their thirties, parents of four children. They are the type of people we often assume have it all together. You would never guess that a longing for love nearly cost them everything.

Jeremy always had a special relationship with his grandpa. They both loved baseball, and his grandpa made it a point to never miss one of Jeremy's games. Jeremy was an exceptional athlete who excelled in baseball and was drafted by the Chicago White Sox. Instead of signing with the Sox, though, Jeremy chose to accept a scholarship to play baseball in college.

Sadly, when Jeremy was halfway through college, his grandpa suddenly died, leaving Jeremy devastated and feeling alone. The one person in the world who he believed loved him unconditionally was now gone. It was then that Jeremy lost touch with God. He felt that God had forgotten about him, so he figured he might as well forget about God.

Trying to fill the void left by his grandfather's death started him on a downward path. His grades began to suffer, and he eventually lost his baseball scholarship and dropped out of college. It seemed to him that he had disappointed everyone.

Jeremy next went through two failed marriages. While going through the second divorce, he watched his mom suffer with breast cancer. Jeremy said, "I wanted nothing to do with God because he showed no signs of wanting anything to do with me. He just seemed to take away anyone who ever got close to me."

Ready to end it all, he swallowed a bottle of pills. Thankfully, his attempt to kill himself failed. But he woke up in a hospital and wondered what had become of his life.

Melissa has a similar story of being driven to a point of desperation because of troubled relationships. Her story begins long before she met Jeremy.

She would tell you that she remembers seldom thinking about God as a child. But after her parents separated when she was a teen, she prayed to anyone out there who would listen. Trying to fill the void that was left by a broken family, she started experimenting with drugs. That, of course, didn't satisfy her deep longings, so she turned to men, hoping they would meet her need. After a painful divorce from a man who mistreated her, she entered into another, even more abusive relationship. She said, "I could never understand why God couldn't stop me from getting beat up. So instead of turning to God, I turned to cocaine."

She met Jeremy when both of them were trying to figure out what to do with the rest of their lives. Speaking for both of them, Jeremy told me, "You could feel the darkness. In spite of finding each other, we were still lost and alone, and we couldn't find our way. We knew our only way out was to admit that we couldn't do it on our own."

It wasn't long after they met that they actively began their search for something more. Their search eventually led them to a church where people were genuinely asking God to make himself real to them. Jeremy and Melissa decided to make the wager as well.

And things began to change for the better. In time, they chose to get baptized as an indication of their newfound spiritual reality. With tears in his eyes, Jeremy's father said to him at his baptism, "I've never been more proud of you than I am right now."

Jeremy told me, "That was the first time I'd seen my dad cry since the day I lost my baseball scholarship."

As they continue to deepen their relationship with God, Melissa and Jeremy know they dare not try to do it alone. They have joined a small group of people who are trying to know God better, just as they are. Melissa remarked, "What keeps us close to God is having each other and having other people in our lives who are on the same journey."

WE LONG FOR LOVE FROM GOD

Longing for love from other people is a good thing, even if relationships can sometimes go terribly wrong. But our need for human connection often obscures a deeper longing. Not only do we have a longing to love and be loved by other people, we also long to love and be loved by God.

A friend of mine was dating a woman who called herself an atheist, and yet she said this: "When I get really down, I tell myself God loves me. Which is interesting, considering I don't believe God exists. Actually, what I tell myself is that God is in love with me."

Fascinating, huh? She has a longing to be loved by a God she doesn't think exists!

Look what John, one of Jesus's closest friends, says about God:

God is love.[23]

What we long for, God doesn't just *have* but actually God *is.* He is love. Furthermore, he pursues us with his love. Here is what John wrote in the same context:

This is love: not that we loved God, but that he loved us and
sent his Son as an atoning sacrifice for our sins.[24]

God's pursuit of us has a name, and the person with that name didn't just walk around talking about love—he lived it so that we can have it. God reaches out to us in Jesus.

Maybe you're reading this and thinking, *You don't know the mess I'm in. You don't know the relational wreckage I have in my past. You don't know how hard I've tried or the disappointment I've experienced in relationships over and over again.* You're right, I don't. But I have a hunch that, one way or another, you're not going to stop trying to find love. Deep in your heart you know it's your inheritance—and you're going to keep pursuing it.

If you're feeling discouragement in your love relationships today, consider these encouraging words from the apostle Paul: "God has poured out his love into our hearts by the Holy Spirit, whom he has given us."[25] God is saying that when your heart feels empty and out of love, if you'll let him he will pour his love into your heart. The result is that not only do you feel his love deep inside your heart, you also have a source of love that gives you what you need to love others the way he loves you.

In the film *Marvin's Room,* Meryl Streep plays a woman named Lee whose pursuit of love has been a disaster. While chasing men in bad relationship after bad relationship, she has neglected her family and alienated her son. When she learns that her sister, Bessie, played by Diane Keaton, has been diagnosed with leukemia, she goes to be tested as a bone-marrow donor. Bessie never married and has spent most of her adult life caring for her bedridden father and senile aunt, who no longer even recognize her.

When Bessie hears that the leukemia is terminal, she breaks down crying. Then she says, "I love them so much."

Lee replies to Bessie, "They love you very much."

Then Bessie says, "That's not what I mean. No, no . . . I mean that I love *them.* I've been so lucky to be able to love someone so much."[26]

Will you open yourself up to letting God fill your longing to love and be loved? In the next chapter you will discover how to express God's love in ways that bring new purpose and direction to your life.

5

What on Earth Am I Here For?

If you're like me, you know deep inside that you are definitely *not* here on earth just for days of ho-hum, yada-yada-yada, more of the same—and then start over again! You feel happiest when you know your life matters.

Sure, this longing for purpose can drive us to do desperate things. But the Creator put the drive in us for our good and the good of others—to make a difference in our world, to reach for greatness, to experience personal fulfillment. And this same longing can help us find our way home to God.

Even when we were kids, that longing was there. Let me show you what I mean.

Think back to when you were a child, maybe five, six, or seven years old. What did you want to be when you grew up? Did you want to be a doctor or a nurse? How about a teacher? Or a professional athlete? Maybe an astronaut or a firefighter? Did you dream of becoming a rock star?

Now ask yourself why in the world you were dreaming about having any kind of job or profession at all. You didn't need a job at that age. You didn't need to take on more responsibility or pay the bills. You were still learning the alphabet and how to write your name correctly! Why even *think* about what you wanted to be when you grew up?

Yet already you had a desire to accomplish something in the world. Erwin McManus put it this way in his book *Soul Cravings:*

We cannot live the life of our dreams without an irrational sense of destiny. . . .

    All of us long to become something more than we are. We are driven to achieve, moved to accomplish, fueled by ambition. It burns hotter in some than in others, but it is within all of us. We're all searching for our unique purpose, our divine destiny.[27]

We're often told that life is the result of one big cosmic accident, that we're the product of billions of years of chance occurrences. Let me ask you, Which do you wish were true: that you were an accident or that you were created for a purpose? I don't think anyone wants to go through life thinking he or she is just a random blip on the radar screen of the universe.

In the Old Testament, God spoke to a man named Jeremiah, revealing how he had hard-wired personal significance into this man from the beginning:

Before I shaped you in the womb,
    I knew all about you.
Before you saw the light of day,
    I had holy plans for you.[28]

What's your gut-level reaction to those words? I suspect that, even if you're not sure there really is a God, even if you believe life is a cosmic accident, something inside you hopes those words are true. It would feel really good to know that—just like Jeremiah—you are here on earth for a reason.

Of course, that belief takes a beating some days. Even for the famous and successful.

"SOMETHING GREATER OUT THERE"

Steve Kroft interviewed quarterback Tom Brady for the news show *60 Minutes* not long after Brady won his third Super Bowl championship with the New England Patriots. At one point in the interview, Brady spoke about his search for fulfillment:

> **Kroft:** This whole experience—this whole upward trajectory—what have you learned about yourself? What kind of an effect does it have on you?
>
> **Brady:** Well, I put incredible amounts of pressure on me. When you feel like you're ultimately responsible for everyone and everything . . . there's a lot of pressure. . . . Why do I have three Super Bowl rings, and still think there's something greater out there for me? I mean, maybe a lot of people would say, "Hey man, this is what [it] is." I reached my goal, my dream, my life. Me, I think: *God, it's gotta be more than this. . . .* (Italics added)
>
> **Kroft:** What's the answer?
>
> **Brady:** I wish I knew. I wish I knew.[29]

In spite of his incredible accomplishments, resulting in significant wealth and fame, Tom Brady was looking for something more. At least on that day.

If our pursuit of success is focused on pleasing someone other than God, we *will* find ourselves looking for something more.

Media mogul and former Atlanta Braves owner Ted Turner grew up in a home with a father who was manic-depressive and struggled with alcoholism. Turner's dad was a stern disciplinarian who thought withholding affection would lead his son to work harder and ultimately succeed.

Almost twenty years after his father committed suicide, Turner was giving a speech. Right in the middle of it, he stopped and pulled out a copy of *Success Magazine* with his picture on the cover. He looked toward the sky and whispered, "Is this enough for you, Dad?"[30]

For many of us, success may not be the issue. The relentless demands of everyday life keep us from finding our true calling.

Ever hear anybody say, "You're going to work yourself to death"? Apparently it can actually happen. Recently, a Bank of America intern in London was found dead in his apartment. After working day and night for weeks, he collapsed in the shower and died of an epileptic seizure.[31]

You might feel that what's keeping you from discovering your true purpose is the drudgery of everyday life: the need to pay the bills, get stuff done, punch in and punch out.

A friend of mine, Mike Breaux, was complaining about how he has to do the same old stuff every day. He explained it this way: "You get up at the same old time, walk into the same old bathroom, look at the same old face in the same old mirror, get in the same old shower, dry off with the same old towel, and put on the same old clothes. You walk down to the same old kitchen, get out the same old bowl, eat the same old cereal, drink the same old coffee, kiss good-bye the same old wife." (*He* said that, not me!)

Then he said, "You drive the same old car down the same old street to the same old job and laugh at the same old jokes the same old boss tells the same old way. You clock out at the same old time, get back in the same old car and drive down that same old street, pull in the same old garage, hug the same old kids, walk into the same old kitchen, and sit down to eat the same old dinner."

Finally Mike said, "You sit in the same old recliner, watch the same old TV show, fall asleep in that same old chair, have to get up and crawl into the same old bed, ask the same old wife the same old question, get the same old answer, roll over, set the same old alarm clock and get up the next day—and do the same old things all over again!"

Are you in the grind of the "same old, same old"? I know you have to pay the bills and take care of your responsibilities. But if you keep doing what you are doing, you are going to keep getting what you've always gotten.

It's not difficult to understand why we can feel a deep disillusionment that causes us to wonder, *Is this all there is? Is this what I worked so hard for all these years? There's got to be more!*

And there is. It starts with the truth about your true value and purpose.

YOU ARE A PIECE OF WORK

The lost son in Jesus's story made "wild living" his goal. (A lot of us went through that phase.) But the son found out eventually that making fun an end in itself was responsible for a lot of the emptiness he wound up feeling.

Fulfillment doesn't come from self-absorbed pursuits. It comes from doing something that has meaning beyond ourselves.

Just as God knew Jeremiah "in the womb," God knew you before you were conceived, and he's had special, sacred plans for your life from before you were even born. These words from the apostle Paul inspire me to climb out of the "same old, same old" every time I hear them:

We are [God's] workmanship, created in Christ Jesus for good works, which God prepared beforehand so that we would walk in them.[32]

Let's break that down:

First that word "workmanship." In the original language it is the word *poiema* (pronounced poy-eh-ma). What English word does that sound like? *Poem,* right? It's an artistic term. It conveys the idea that you are not mass produced. God made you individually, uniquely, poetically. God is saying, "You're a piece of work!" You may have had others say that to you in the past, but did you ever think they were paying you a compliment? When God says, "You are a piece of work!" he is saying that he personally created you and crafted you, that you are a work of art.

You're not a work of art to simply hang on the wall for somebody to admire. You are artwork "created for good works." In other words, God is saying that he created you with a purpose, to do good works that are aligned with the greater good he wants to do in this world. So the "good works" you are created to do are all about accomplishing what God put you here to do and purposed for you to do from the beginning! That's part of your inheritance.

So go ahead and say it out loud, "There's got to be more." God himself placed that desire inside you, and as you find your way back to him, he will show you the unique and purposeful life he created you for. You'll know you're finding it when you see a life that is about more than just you.

WHERE JOY MEETS THE WORLD'S NEED

Several years ago I had dinner with my friend and mentor Bob Buford. For much of his life, Bob ran a successful cable television company. After his son, Ross, tragically died, Bob came to a point in his life he called "Halftime." He wrote a book by that title that tells how he moved from focusing on success to focusing on significance. What Bob said at dinner has stayed with me ever since: "One of people's great fears is running out of money, but that's not their *greatest* fear. Another significant fear people have is the fear of dying, but that's not people's *greatest* fear either." He paused and said, "Deep down, our single *greatest* fear is to live a life of insignificance, to come to the end of our life and feel like we never really did anything that mattered. That is our *greatest* fear."

Are you feeling like you are stuck in the same old, same old? Do you have a gut feeling that there's got to be more? Author and theologian Frederick Buechner points us in the right direction when he says, "The place God calls you to is the place where your deep gladness and the world's deep hunger meet."[33]

You can't get there on your own. But if you will travel with me on this journey to God, he will bring you to that intersection of your joy and the world's need. Such is the power of longing turned toward God.

In the next chapter, we get to another type of longing—the longing to make sense of life. To know that there's meaning, not only when life is going our way, but even when it's going very wrong indeed.

6

Those Unanswered "Why" Questions

A company that sells educational curricula says that if you're going to be a good parent or teacher, you need to be prepared to answer children's *why* questions. Here are some of the *why* questions they suggest you be prepared to answer:

Why do I have a shadow?

Why does the wind blow?

Why do balls bounce?

Why does your breath smell so bad, Daddy?

Why is Grandpa's hair gray?

Why is Grandma's hair blue?

Why do camels have humps?

Why do dogs bark?

Why do cats have whiskers?

For the low, low price of $19.95, this company will send you a curriculum that will answer all your kids' why questions.

Regardless of our age, we all have an insatiable appetite for the question, Why? As adults, our why questions just become more complicated. *Why didn't God heal him? Why did she have to leave? Why did my most cherished dream have to die?*

I imagine that when the son in Jesus's story blew his inheritance and his adventure turned sour, his situation must have left him with some questions. A famine struck the land, and he had no money or food. "So he went and hired himself out to a citizen of that country, who sent him to his fields to feed pigs. He longed to fill his stomach with the pods that the pigs were eating, but no one gave him anything."[34] At that point his situation must have left him asking, *Why didn't this turn out like I thought it would? Why am I so lonely, broke, and empty? Why did this journey end up with me in a place like this?*

Our anger, disappointment, and sorrow related to the why questions can drive us away from God—get us lost, make us forget. In fact, Jon and I have discovered that, perhaps more than any other longing, it's the whys that keep people at a distance from God.

But there's good news too. This same deeply felt need for fairness, goodness, and healing can also help us close the distance and reconnect in faith with God.

IF GOD IS ALL POWERFUL AND ALL LOVING . . .

One of the most challenging questions we will ask as we find our way back to God is this one: "Why does God allow suffering?"

After a tsunami hit Southeast Asia, killing over a quarter million people, more than one person must have wondered aloud, "If God is all powerful and all loving, he should have stopped the tsunami from happening, but he didn't. So either he *could* have and he *didn't*, or he *wanted* to but *couldn't*. You can't have it both ways." This is not only a big philosophical and theological question. It is also a personal question.

Rick's earliest memories are of him, his sister, and his mom getting beaten by his dad. Then, in an entirely unexpected turn of events, when Rick was eight years old, his dad chose to follow Jesus and became a different person. Ironically, this change in his dad's life caused Rick to turn away from God. He said, "I actually began to hate God. I couldn't understand how he could forgive my dad after all he'd done to us."

His resentments burning, Rick wandered further and further from God. But his hate and anger weren't directed only toward God. He would tell you there were only a handful of people he didn't detest.

One of those people was Mandy. There was something special about her. Rick said, "I noticed that when Mandy prayed she actually believed she was talking to God and she would see real stuff happen. She began to rekindle my hope in God, and she helped me understand why God would forgive my dad."

Eventually Rick married his friend Mandy. Their "in sickness and in health" vow was put to the test sooner than anyone could have anticipated. Just six hours after their wedding ceremony, Mandy suffered a stroke and was rushed to the hospital. Rick recalls, "I spent my wedding night in my car in the parking lot of a hospital, sobbing uncontrollably, asking God why. 'Why today? Why ever? Why us? What are you doing, God?'"

He got only silence in response.

LOSING WALT

While writing this book, I came face to face with some of my own unanswered why questions.

For several years I watched my father-in-law, Walt, struggle with the demon of dementia. In the early stages I sat across the room and watched him hold his head in his hands and ask out loud in anguish, "Why can't I get my brain to work?" Later my wife, Sue, would get phone calls from him with fictional concerns that ranged from his second-floor apartment flooding with water, to running out of money, to the royal family showing up when he had nothing to feed them. Each of his fears was a trick that the disease was playing on the mind of this good man.

Walt wasn't just my father-in-law. He was also a great father to my wife, a model grandparent to my kids, and someone I loved. He and his wife of fifty-seven years, Lola, never missed spending either Christmas or Easter with us nor forgot any of our kids' birthdays. He was a successful salesman, always generous; he even gave us a check for the down payment on our first house.

And now he was being tortured by dementia. It hurt me. It was terrible for my wife. It left us both asking God, "Why do you allow this kind of pain?" and "Why him?" It got to the point where we began to pray, "God, if you are not going to heal Walt, just take him." It felt like God wasn't there or *was* there and didn't care.

Walt's gone now. He's in heaven, where his mind works perfectly, and we're happy for him. But to be honest, the rest of us in the family are still left wondering, *Why did he have to go through all that?*

NOT THE WAY IT WAS MADE

When we ask, "Why does God allow suffering?" we are saying that a loving God wouldn't make a world with so much hurt in it. And on that point, we are absolutely correct. The suffering we see in the news every day and know from personal experience is not the world as God created it.

As I mentioned before, the creation account contained in Genesis states, "God saw all that he had made, and it was very good."[35] God made the world good, and "good" in this instance means without flaw or defect. No sickness. No suffering. No death. No sadness. No loneliness. No violence. That's the world God made, yet we know that people all over this world aren't experiencing a life they would describe as "good."

Why?

In the movie *Bruce Almighty*, Bruce, played by Jim Carrey, is angry about the way his life is going and blames God. God, played by Morgan Freeman, gives Bruce godlike powers.

Initially, Bruce enjoys his newfound power, and soon he is exploiting his abilities for his own gain. But in time he realizes that making decisions on a godlike scale is complicated.

In his frustration at trying to recapture the love of his girlfriend, Grace, he poses this question to God: "How do you make so many people love you without affecting free will?"

God responds: "Welcome to my world, son. When you come up with an answer to that one, you let me know."[36]

Truth is, there are no easy answers to suffering. The philosophers know it, Wall Street traders know it, and so does the guy down at the car wash. One entire book in the Bible (Job) grapples with the question of why bad things happen to good people, and God's answers to Job are almost entirely posed as—maybe you guessed it—more questions.[37]

So we need to proceed here with humility and sensitivity. If you had cancer, you wouldn't appreciate a visitor who showed up at your hospital room while you're being prepped for chemo and said, "Cheer up, kiddo. Everything's going to be just fine." And you shouldn't believe two pastors from Chicago if they say they have a lock on the answer to suffering and evil in the world.

But let's dig deeper.

FREEDOM TO CHOOSE

When God made us, he didn't make us to be puppets or robots. Our loving God, who wants us to love him in return, created the world without suffering, but we know that there simply cannot be authentic love without choice and freedom. He gave us the choice to find our way back to him, but he doesn't force himself on us. He has always given us the freedom to choose to love and follow him or choose not to love and follow him.

Sadly, humankind turned away from our heavenly Father, and when they did, all hell broke loose. The result was relational strife and spiritual disruption. The apostle Paul mentions that even creation began to decay as a result of humankind's decision to turn away from God.[38]

When the first humans rejected God, God himself asked, "What is this you have done?"[39] He wasn't asking because he didn't know what they had done. Of course he knew. He asked, "What have you done?" out of disappointment, in the same way a father of teenagers would ask the question when returning home to find the house a mess.

The hard truth is that most human suffering is directly or indirectly the result of human choice going against the way God made the world. Whenever anyone is victimized by abuse, crime, war, or violence, somebody somewhere is going against God's ways and against his dream for this world.

You might hear that and think, *But what about suffering that isn't caused by human choice? What about famines like the one in Somalia in 2011?* It was believed to be the worst drought in Africa in sixty years. As many as 11 million people were at risk of severe malnutrition or starving to death. So we might ask, "Why doesn't God just make it rain and put an end to the starvation? Just a snap of his fingers is all it would take."

The reality is that the drought wasn't the only cause of the starvation. There is more than enough food produced on our planet to supply every single one of the earth's more than 7 billion inhabitants with almost three thousand calories a day. Food scarcity is not the real problem.

The real problem that keeps food from getting to places where people are starving is a combination of political corruption, greed, and ignorance. These are the results of turning away from God. He made the world the way we think a loving God *should* have made it. The vast majority of the suffering around us today is the result of our actions since then.

WHY DOESN'T GOD FIX IT?

The natural follow-up question is this: "God *could* fix it, so why *doesn't* he?" And the truth is, he *is* in the process of fixing it. He is at work through great organizations and nonprofits all over the world. He is also at work through good-hearted individuals and communities of faith. The church's mission is about reaching people who are far from God, and it's also about seeking to restore God's dream for the world and everyone in it.

When you see people in a vibrant faith family actively engaged in their community, you're not just seeing people help provide kids with lunches, school supplies, and shoes. They are also working to restore God's dream for the world. They aren't just doing some good, charitable activities. They are choosing to be part of restoring the world to something like what it was in the beginning and will be when Jesus returns to completely restore this world to its original intent. God did not give up on his vision for this world, and we don't need to either.

LET'S GET PERSONAL

I hope some of what you've read to this point has begun to chisel away at the mountain of questions regarding why a good God allows so much pain and suffering in our world. But a more personal, and possibly more painful, question remains: How do we deal with the toll that our own suffering can take on our journey to God? In other words, how do you not let your own suffering or the suffering around you keep you stuck in the questions, unable to move forward?

If you don't believe there is a God because of suffering you see or your own personal experience, I can understand that. But if there is no God, who's to say suffering is wrong and shouldn't exist? In other words, if the world is just one big meaningless cosmic accident and life is simply survival of the fittest, then why would those who suffer have the sense that something is wrong or that suffering shouldn't exist?

There is a reason you feel like your life and the world aren't the way they are supposed to be. There is a reason your suffering feels not just painful but also wrong and unfair. *God gave you those feelings.* Your desire to see wrongs righted and reach an end to suffering is part of your inheritance as a child of God.

SEEING A GOOD GOD IN HIS PEOPLE

To this day, Rick says that he has no real answer to his why question: "Why would God allow my wife to suffer a stroke on our wedding night?" But Rick will also tell you that, even in the midst of the most unimaginable crisis, God made himself real. Rick said, "When I finally got out of the car and walked back into the hospital on my wedding night, I found seventy of my closest friends and family in the waiting room, all there to support me. A few friends brought guitars, and before I knew it, there was an all-out worship and prayer session going on in the waiting room and hallway."

The road to recovery was a hard one for Mandy and Rick, but God continues to show his love to them. People have paid for their rent, medical bills, cell phone service, food, car insurance, therapy, and date nights. Rick says the experience has actually deepened his faith in God.

Rick told Jon, "After seeing God move so clearly through his people, I know three things for certain: In spite of my inability to understand him, God is wise and *knows* what is best. He is generous and *gives* us what is best. And he is loving and *does* what is best. Though I can't say that I know exactly why God would allow all this to happen to me, I can say that, having lived through it, I wouldn't trade knowing that God is unequivocally good for having a more comfortable honeymoon. As hard as it was, it gave us a gift that can't be taken away."

DRAWING NEAR

Dietrich Bonhoeffer, a German theologian and pastor imprisoned by the Nazis, wrote these words from his prison cell: "Only the suffering God can help."[40] Jesus's suffering on the cross may not give us the reason for our pain and suffering, but I believe it tells us what the reason is *not*. The reason is not that God doesn't love us. The cross upon which Jesus died, as awful as it was, demonstrates God's love for the world. The cross says that God is not uncaring, God is not indifferent. The cross means Jesus went through the ultimate suffering for us.

I've come to find great comfort in Bonhoeffer's words. He knew that, even if there is no obvious answer to an unjust imprisonment or to a good man's tormenting dementia or to any other suffering that comes our way, God is with us in Jesus and provides a way through it.

I don't know what pain you're going through. And I don't pretend to have answers for all of life's suffering. My prayer is that, as you find your way back to God, you, too, will look to the cross and see God, through Jesus, entering into our suffering to bring good from it.

Pain and suffering make it seem God is not there, that God doesn't care. But Jesus understands that. He came to earth to live out in the flesh the truth of who God is and how he, too, feels about the unanswerable questions we face in life. Most of all, he came to show us that these same questions are meant to draw us nearer to God rather than push us further away.

There's got to be more. That's the instinctive reaction to a life apart from God. Our longing for something more, something better will drive us closer to God, if we'll let it. He's what's missing in our lives.

And the next step beyond that realization is a desire to see real change take place inside us.

AWAKENING TO REGRET:
"I wish I could start over."

He came to his senses.
—Luke 15:17

7

Zoe Kind of Life

In the first awakening, we found a young traveler who thought he knew what he wanted. It was simple—a longing for something better, something more exciting, something more fulfilling than what he had back home with Dad. And he planned to chase it as long and far as necessary to find it.

Do you recognize the intense longing that was driving him? I do. I've heard myself say it many times: "There's got to be more!"

Trying to fulfill that longing had taken him away from home and into the good life. And let's be honest. It. Was. Fun. *Fabulous!*

At first.

But something happened. Things took a turn. The party lights went out, and all he had left in the morning was a room full of empties and a phone number written on the mirror with lipstick. And an awful emptiness inside. The life he wanted turned out to be the life he hated.

Then he went broke.

The young man got so desperate that he hired himself out to feed the pigs. He got so hungry that the slop he was throwing to the pigs started looking tasty. But he wasn't even allowed to eat the pigs' food.

That's what you call "hitting bottom." And for the young man, "bottom" was the place where things began to turn.

In the words of Jesus's story, "He came to his senses." Once again, he was waking up. Do you see it? The first time he had awakened to a longing for more. This time he woke up to a longing for something else entirely.

When he came to his senses, he said, "How many of my father's hired servants have food to spare, and here I am starving to death!"[41]

What he realized now was how desperately he wanted to go back home and start over! But how could he? He had already taken his share of home and squandered every last dollar of it.

This brings us to the second awakening—the next in our significant breakthroughs in our journey back to God. Jon and I call it the *awakening to regret.*

You look at your life one bleak morning and realize that, for all your best efforts, you've made a mess of things. You're filled with disappointment and remorse. And now that you see things more clearly, you'd love another chance. But you're not sure you have it coming.

Come to think of it, why would you?

But stay with us.

"I Wish I Could Start Over"

Inside each of us is the conviction that we came from goodness and love and that we're made for more of it. When we hit bottom and realize what a mess we have made of this life, and what a mess life has made of us, our reaction is to say, "I wish I could start over."

Could it be that you are experiencing an awakening to regret? Do you want to start over now?

You can start over. Your intuition about your origins in goodness and love is absolutely correct. And God can allow you to start over again.

The next step in your spiritual journey is to say this prayer:

God, if you are real,
make yourself real to me.
Awaken in me the possibility
that with you I could start over again.

Start your day with this prayer. End your day with this prayer. Let every twinge of regret and pang of remorse become fuel for your starting-over prayer. Say it as often as it comes to mind. God is listening. So keep praying.

Keep reading too. You are about to make an astonishing discovery.

Most of us, when we're ready to start over, simply want to go back to the life we had before everything went south. But God has other ideas. He doesn't just want to help us get back to that better life as we imagine it when we're surrounded by pigs.

He wants us to experience a different kind of life altogether.

WHEN *BIOS* MET *ZOE*

I often hear people describe their journey back to God as "life changing." That is exactly what God promises us—a change in the kind of life we experience.

Jesus explained to his followers that finding your way back to God is life changing. It's not just your future that changes but your past and your present as well. Speaking of people who know and love him, Jesus said,

I have come that they may have life, and have it to the full.[42]

That is exactly what can happen for you! Life change.

The original language of the New Testament has two words for life. One is the word *bios*. It's the root word for *biology*. Bios means "natural life." It can also refer to a chronological life. The average lifetime includes 250,000 hours of sleep, 76,000 meals, and 200,000 trips to the bathroom. All of that is a part of a bios life.

But there's another word for life in the Bible, and it's the word *zoe*. Zoe includes a bios kind of life but goes way beyond that. Bios is about quantity, but zoe is about a quality of life that comes only from knowing God. A zoe life ultimately refers to eternal life, the kind of life that you were made for and that will never end.

When Jesus says, "I have come that they may have life," guess which word for life he uses? Right, *zoe!* Jesus is talking about a quality of life with God that changes your past, present, and future. When you find your way back to God, you discover the zoe life.

"Now I Can Go On"

Eileen cried every day. Every day of her adult life for years she mourned the decision she had made during her first marriage to have an abortion. In her tears she wondered who her child might have become. She had two beautiful children from a second marriage but still found it impossible to forgive herself or to talk about what she had done. She was tortured by that secret. It was a grieving that wouldn't subside.

Eileen's awakening to an understanding that she could truly start over helped her find her way back to God. She discovered zoe life, a quality of life where there is grace and forgiveness from God for whatever is in our past.

The biblical hero David, awakened to the regret in his own life, wrote about the forgiveness God offers:

> *His unfailing love toward those who fear him*
>   *is as great as the height of the heavens above the earth.*
> *He has removed our sins as far from us*
>   *as the east is from the west.*[43]

In finding God, Eileen found grace for her past and hope that one day she will meet her first child in heaven. Those gifts have transformed her past and what it was doing to her.

"I've realized that with God, my mistakes of the past are put away. It's not that they didn't happen or they don't matter. It's that God has dealt with them and now I can go on to better things."

These days, Eileen's tears have subsided, and she now tells her story to help others experience that life-changing forgiveness. God has a way of doing that with even our worst messes—the very messes that have been keeping us from approaching him.

SOME OF THE BEST STUFF IN LIFE

If you're a coffee fanatic, you might know that the most expensive coffee in the world is *kopi luwak*. It once came exclusively from Indonesia. Kopi luwak is considered the most exotic, complex-tasting coffee in the world, and it is definitely the most costly! Think your local café is expensive? This coffee can cost $300 or more a pound.

The kopi luwak coffee bean also has an interesting story. *Kopi* is the Indonesian word for "coffee," and *luwak* is the name of a small Indonesian catlike animal, a civet, that comes out only at night. The luwak eats the finest coffee berries at night and then digests them while sleeping during the day. In the morning the locals harvest these beans from the luwak's excrement. Yep, every single kopi luwak bean passes through the digestive tract of an Indonesian civet until it comes out the other end!

Remember, kopi luwak not only is the most expensive coffee in the world but also is considered by many to be the most exquisite coffee in the world. I tell you this as a reminder that some of the best stuff in life comes from crap!

What crap do you have in your life? The Bible tells us that God is giving the world a fresh start by offering forgiveness of sins. Give all your crap to God, and he will let you start over by turning it into something extraordinary.

THE PASTOR WHO LOST HIS RELIGION

As a young man, Rich was part of a Christian family and went to church regularly. From an early age, he felt God calling him to be a pastor. So he did what wannabe pastors usually do—he got theological training, earned his chops in church ministry, and eventually worked his way to the role of senior pastor. He was so successful in his ministry profession that two of the churches he led were big enough to be described as "mega." Along the way, Rich married a woman who was good at fulfilling the traditional role of a pastor's wife, and the two of them had a couple of kids. Everything seemed to be going great, just as Rich had envisioned back when he was a young man.

But then his life took a detour that Rich never saw coming.

Rich was vaguely aware that he'd become complacent in his marriage, but he couldn't believe it when his wife told him that she was leaving him. Speaking for herself and the kids, she told him, "We can do just fine without you." And with that she was gone. In practically no time, she was remarried to someone else, and another man was raising Rich's kids.

Rich lost his family.

He lost his home.

He lost his job and his career.

He lost his financial security.

He lost his identity.

He didn't quite lose his faith in God, but he certainly felt estranged from God in a way he had never experienced before.

During this time, as Rich put it, anger toward his ex-wife became his "drug of choice," and he was addicted to it. He was mad at God too. "I could feel my heart growing ever harder, ever colder, ever darker," he recalled. He was a "practical atheist," he said, living as if God did not exist. He was simply living for Rich. A new job in retail sales management kept him afloat financially and provided some temporary purpose for his days, yet he knew that this new existence was not what he'd been made for.

If anyone ever needed to start over, it was Rich.

He knew he needed help, so he began praying, and he asked others to pray for him as well. "God was patient and gracious with me," Rich says, "proving himself the faithful God he is. Through a series of twists and turns in my story, God has gradually restored that irrevocable sense of calling to something more."

Rich is rebuilding his relationship with God on a new and more genuine basis. Along with the rebuilding has come a desire to minister to others again.

He says, "I am not proud of how low I sank or how fast I slid to the bottom of the barrel. But I know God is going to take that mess of my life and make it a message—a message that helps others in the middle of their own messes find hope at the end of their rope. That's what he did for me."

God Can Change Your Now

When you make the wager with God to show himself as real, sometimes life change happens slowly and other times all at once. Either way, it's the jump-start to a new kind of existence. And it can happen in the most unexpected ways, to the most unpromising people.

CBS *Evening News* told a story about an anonymous businessman who travels the country every Christmas giving away tens of thousands of dollars of his own money, $100 at a time, to people he doesn't know.[44] He finds people in bus stations and thrift stores and hands them a hundred-dollar bill as a Christmas gift. The reactions vary from "Are you lying?" and "I can't take this" to "This is the nicest thing that has ever happened to me!"

For Thomas Coates, this generous act was life changing. Thirty-year-old Coates was a heroin addict, a total deadbeat, and a dad who had hocked his son's toys for drug money. He admitted he didn't understand why his girlfriend hadn't left him and taken their son with her.

Instead his girlfriend suggested that he pray to God. She said, "I know you don't really believe in him, but maybe you can try it." Tom prayed for the first time since childhood. He said a simple, desperate prayer, with little faith that it would change anything.

Then when Tom was sitting by himself in a bus station, a stranger gave him two one-hundred-dollar bills.

Tom looked up in shock, saying, "I didn't earn that."

The stranger persisted, "You deserve it. You are a good man, I can tell."

Tom had not heard those kinds of affirming words since his mom spoke them when he was a kid. Then the stranger patted him on the back and said, "See you, pal," and left as quickly as he had shown up. Tom had called himself an atheist, but the timing of his prayer and this outsider's generosity were too much to dismiss. With tears flowing, Tom confessed, "It's just amazing. That was a miracle. God was saying to me, 'Do you believe me now?'"

Tom's life had been mired in longing and regret. But in one moment he went from a bios life where he lived one empty day after another trying to satisfy his drug addiction, to a zoe kind of life believing there was a God who would give him another chance. God's response to Tom's prayer convinced him he could start over. Tom checked himself into a treatment facility, and he said, "This will be the first time with God at the helm."

LIFE THAT'S ABOUT *LIFE!*

If Tom was a deadbeat, Scott and Kirsten were overachievers. They both had graduate degrees, were making the kind of money that put them in the top 1 percent, and lived with their two sons in a community that was deemed "the best community in the United States to raise a family." They thought they had figured out what life was all about. But they were living a bios kind of life, just one day after another that offered no purpose or cause bigger than themselves or their suburban home. The disillusionment became disappointment, and the disappointment grew into a deep depression and regret. Something had to change.

In a moment of prayer, these words came into Kirsten's mind: "I was hungry and you gave me nothing to eat, I was thirsty and you gave me nothing to drink, I was a stranger and you did not invite me in, I needed clothes and you did not clothe me, I was sick and in prison and you did not look after me."[45] The words were from a story Jesus told. It spurred Kirsten and her husband to start talking about what a change in priority might look like in their lives.

Over the next five years, they sold their home, changed jobs, and moved into an under-resourced neighborhood to live alongside people who are marginalized and forgotten. Scott became a schoolteacher in a poorly performing elementary school. Kirsten launched a thriving compassion and justice nonprofit that mobilizes thousands of volunteers. One of the most significant risks they took was moving their two elementary-age boys into a school district with a bare-bones budget, few extracurricular activities, and a growing gang problem. Scott and Kirsten will tell you that their boys have thrived. In Kirsten's words, "We thought we were making sacrifices, but the truth is, we are living a better life now than ever before!"

In his book *The Irresistible Revolution,* Shane Claiborne says that the question of life after death is still significant, but what people are wondering most about is "whether there is life *before* death."[46] What Kirsten and Scott discovered is a zoe kind of life, a life before death. A life that has purpose. A life with a cause. It's a life that gets you out of bed in the morning because you know that you have something important to contribute to the world.

Finding your way back to God offers you a zoe kind of life.

A CALL ON CHRISTMAS

The zoe life that God offers us is never ending, both historically and personally. It started with him before time and goes on with him after time. This was never more apparent to me than a few years ago on Christmas Day.

That year, Christmas fell on a Sunday, so my family went to church in the morning, and then we came home to unwrap our gifts together. For me, there was something about the combination of the celebration at church on Christmas Day and the rush of enthusiastic kids opening presents that made Christmas extra wonderful that year.

In the middle of all that Christmas cheer, our phone rang. It was my friend Paul. He and his wife, Jeanne, were both in their early forties and had two middle school–age daughters. "Can you come on over?" he said. "It looks like Jeanne might not make it." Jeanne had been battling cancer for the last four years and had been in hospice care for the last several weeks.

I hurried over. But by the time I got across town, Jeanne had died.

At their home I stood next to Paul, with my arm around his shoulder, looking at Jeanne's lifeless body. To the casual observer, it was over. Jeanne's life had come to an end. And if you were talking about her bios life, you would be right. She had lived the last of her chronological days on this planet. But some years before, Jeanne and Paul had come to know zoe life. As Jesus explains,

> *I am the resurrection and the life. He who believes in me will live,*
> *even though he dies; and whoever lives and believes in me will never*
> *die. Do you believe this?*[47]

Paul and I both knew that death was not the end. Jeanne's life was not over. Yes, her bios life was completed, but her zoe life was continuing in heaven. It's a kind of life that will never end.

Are you tired of living a mere bios life? Are you ready to be done with living out a string of days with pain from the past, no purpose in your present, and no confidence about your future? Your journey away from regret and toward your home in God also takes you toward a deeper, truer life. The life God offers you is a zoe kind of life. It's the kind of life that invites you to start over today and begin living the way God always dreamed you could live . . . forever.

8

How to Start Over

Are you starting to see that the awakening to regret is a huge one? It's about coming to our senses. Waking up to our actual circumstances and realizing we need a change. It can happen in an instant. Suddenly the lights come on, and we realize where our brilliant plans have taken us—and perhaps we see, as if for the first time, that our lives stink. Maybe literally, as in Jesus's story.

And coming "to his senses" is exactly what the young man in the parable did.[48] The next thing he did? He started for home. We know it's true, because a few sentences later Jesus said,

He got up and went.[49]

But wait.

There's a Grand Canyon of a time lapse hiding in there somewhere. Do you see it? It falls right between "came to his senses" and "got up and went." At least for me and most people I know. For months and years, sometimes for a whole lifetime, we *see* that our life's a mess, that things have to change, but we don't *do* anything about it. So we flounder in regret for years. The canyon between desiring to start over and taking that first determined step seems uncrossable.

Maybe you've noticed this problem of "stuckness" in someone you know. Maybe you notice it in you.

Why do some people seem to sincerely *want* to get in motion toward a new life but seem unable to make it happen?

The conundrum of stuckness is what this chapter is about. We'll look at what it takes to start over and why, for every son and daughter of the Father, it's always, always possible—no matter what we've done.

Brennan Manning understood this powerful dynamic better than most. He was a priest and a skid-row alcoholic who became a ragamuffin evangelist telling people about the love of God. Once Jon and I hosted a gathering that was designed to help people find their way back to God, and we asked Manning to speak. He told a story I've never forgotten.

Max Is "a Heckuva Guy"

Manning was at an inpatient rehab center with twenty-five other chemically dependent men, including a guy Manning just called Max.[50] Max was a nominal Christian, married with five kids, owner of his own company, and wealthy. He seemed like a "put together" guy. But he'd been in and out of rehab for years and continued to relapse. Nothing helped.

The counselor was determined that this time was going to be different. On this particular day, he started by asking Max about how much he drank.

Max went into his usual mild-mannered denial, saying that his drinking was normal and he didn't really have a problem.

The group leader interrupted and said, "Where is my phone?" Somebody handed him his phone, and he called a number. When a voice answered on the other end, he put it on speaker. It was the owner of a local tavern Max frequented. The counselor introduced himself and said, "I'm here with Max, and with his family's permission, I am researching his drinking history. Could you tell me approximately how much Max drinks at your place?"

"Oh, Max; he's a heckuva guy, comes in here every day after work. He has five or six drinks a day, sometimes more, and he usually buys rounds for everybody. Everybody loves the guy."

Max heard this and erupted in anger. He started questioning both the integrity and the ancestry of the tavern owner and the counselor. Then he quickly regained his composure and said something about how even Jesus got angry at times.

Then the counselor asked Max, "Has your drinking affected your children? Have you ever been unkind to one of your kids?"

Max said, "I'm glad you brought that up. Two of my sons graduated from Ivy League schools, and Max Junior is in his third year at— "

"I didn't ask you that," the counselor jumped in. "At least once in his life, every father has been unkind to one of his kids. So give us one specific example."

A long pause ensued. Finally Max said, "Well, I was a little thoughtless with my daughter on Christmas Eve."

"What happened?" the counselor asked.

Max said, "I don't remember. I just get this heavy feeling whenever I think about it."

"What happened?"

Max's voice rose in anger. "I told you I don't remember! I'm sure it wasn't that bad."

The counselor called another number. "Good morning, ma'am. This is Max's counselor. We're in the middle of a group session, and your husband just told us that he was unkind to your daughter on Christmas Eve. Can you give me the details, please?"

"It seems like it happened just yesterday," the soft voice said. "Our nine-year-old wanted a new pair of shoes for Christmas, so on the afternoon of the twenty-fourth, Max drove her to the store and told her to get whatever shoes she wanted. When she climbed back into the truck he was driving, she kissed him on the cheek and told him he was the best daddy in the whole world. He was so proud of himself, he decided to celebrate.

"He stopped at the tavern and told our daughter he would be right out. It was an extremely cold day, about twelve below zero. Max left the motor running and locked both doors because he couldn't take our little girl into the bar. He was only going to have one drink. It was a little after three o'clock, and my husband met some old army buddies, lost track of time, and came out of the tavern at midnight, drunk. The truck had stopped running and the windows were frozen shut. Our daughter was badly frostbitten on both ears and on her fingers. When we got her to the hospital, the doctors had to operate. They amputated the thumb and forefinger on her right hand. She will be deaf for the rest of her life."

Max collapsed to the floor, sobbing uncontrollably. Then the counselor surprised everybody in the group by saying this to Max: "There's the door over there. Pack your bags and get out of here. This is rehab for alcoholics, not liars."

After a few moments, Max's sobbing turned into pleading to be allowed to stay in treatment. He began talking at length about what he'd done and how he hated himself for it, and the counselor and the group began to help him work through it. He had come to a place of deep regret, and he knew he needed to start over.

Manning finished the story: "Max proceeded to undergo the most striking personality change I have ever witnessed. He became the most open, sincere, vulnerable, and caring person in the group. He found a real, personal relationship with God, got sober, and stayed sober for the first time in his adult life."

Repent = "I Want to Start Over"

Maybe you can identify with Max or parts of his story. Or maybe your story is not at all like Max's story. It's far less dramatic, perhaps not as painful, but at the same time you know what it means to live with regret—that "heavy feeling," as Max described it. Maybe that heaviness is keeping you at a distance from God. If you are going to find your way back to God, you must have the spiritual awakening that brings you to say, "God, I want to start over." Without this awakening, and the turning that follows, you will continue to sleepwalk through life, unaware of your destructive patterns, big and small. Until you see and move toward the new life that can be yours, you will keep moving toward a life of pain, boredom, and doom.

The one word that best describes this awakening is *repentance.* Unfortunately, the word *repentance* has lost its original meaning and is more associated with street preachers and feeling bad about yourself.

Repentance is not limited to emotions like contrition, guilt, and remorse. Repentance is more about action—it's the starting over that happens as a result of those emotions. The thing is, we can feel bad and wish things were different and still not be repentant.

I've had lots of conversations with people from a variety of religious backgrounds, and one constant I hear is regret. Many people go through their lives consumed with regret. Living and remaining in regret is not from God, and it never has been. Regret is meant to be a starting place—a catalyst for getting us moving.

The New Testament writer Paul, whose past gave him plenty of reasons for regret, put it this way: "Godly sorrow brings repentance that leads to salvation and leaves no regret, but worldly sorrow brings death."[51] Do you see the forward motion in Paul's words? What starts (a) with sorrow and regret leads (b) to repentance, and that leads (c) to salvation—and that leaves sorrow and regret behind. That's why I want you to realize that repentance should never be equated with mere feelings, no matter how sincere.

HOW IT WORKS: REPENTANCE IS MOTION, NOT EMOTION

The Greek word for repent is *metanoia,* and it means to change direction. The *noia* part of the word is the word for "mind." The *meta* part of the word means "to change," as in *metamorphosis.* Put them together, and *metanoia* refers to a significant change of mind or a change of direction. This is not just a tweak or adjustment. This means to be heading in one direction and then do a 180-degree turn and head in the exact opposite direction.

Whenever you think of the word *repentance* from now on, think of it as a turning point. It means to turn from whatever is distracting you or pulling you away from God and to intentionally turn toward God. This is something you will do not once but rather over and over again.

A few years ago, my wife and I spent two days going through a Life-Plan process.[52] In this terrific process, you look at who God made you to be and then you align all your future plans to accomplish the dream God has for your life. One of the important exercises in this process was taking a look at my life and determining key turning points. I was surprised at what surfaced.

There was a track meet in sixth grade where I told myself, *Just work harder and you will win.* It was the last lap, and I was about to lose the lead when those words came to me. In that moment I pushed myself even harder and held on for the win. That was a turning point for me because from then on, I saw hard work as my strategy for success.

Another one was my two days in the hospital with chest pains at the age of twenty-one because I tried taking twenty-seven credit hours in one semester while working a part-time job. That was a turning point where I realized I do have limits.

Then there was the moment my first child was born, and I realized that my life isn't just about me—another turning point.

Turning points change you forever. You are going down a path, and something happens that takes you in a new direction.

Repentance is the realization that the direction you are headed in is taking you far from God and all the good he wants for you. And so you turn from what you were pursuing and turn toward God. In order to find your way to God, you need to do a serious inventory of your life. Ask yourself:

- What do I think about that pulls me away from God?
- What do I indulge in that distracts me from God?
- What do I avoid that could draw me near to God?

Ask others to be brutally honest with you: "What do you see in my life that I need to turn from so I can turn toward God?"

This moment is a turning point for you. Either you will move forward and find your way back to God, or you will retreat, repeat your mistakes, and experience a life of regret. The best choice seems obvious. But making that choice is up to you.

THINKING ABOUT RUMSPRINGA

My daughter, Amy, grew up going to church, but unfortunately it was not always a safe place for her. Some people said things they shouldn't have said or placed unfair expectations on her. With that kind of religious pressure, it was almost impossible for her to feel the love of God from the people she should have felt it from most. She resented the church and felt distant from God.

In a text conversation while I was in a meeting in Miami and she was in class as an undergrad in Grand Rapids, Michigan, she explained to me about rumspringa.

[8:36:51 a.m.] **Amy:** yo

[8:42:33 a.m.] **Dave:** what's up?

[8:42:37 a.m.] **Amy:** nada

[8:42:40 a.m.] **Amy:** just chillin in class

[8:42:51 a.m.] **Dave:** cool. I'm just chillin in one more meeting.

[8:49:39 a.m.] **Amy:** i think i might start going to church again

[8:49:46 a.m.] **Dave:** really?

[8:49:55 a.m.] **Amy:** i feel like the last three years were my rumspringa hahaha

[8:49:56 a.m.] **Dave:** really . . . why?

[8:49:58 a.m.] **Amy:** i love the amish

[8:50:13 a.m.] **Amy:** but for real i think that whole idea is really intriguing

[8:50:16 a.m.] **Dave:** "rumspringa" . . . what is that?

[8:50:56 a.m.] **Amy:** where amish kids get to go check out modern culture and it's not held against them . . .

[8:51:10 a.m.] **Amy:** . . . and then they come back and decide if they want to be a part of the amish church

[8:51:23 a.m.] **Dave:** cool.

[8:51:27 a.m.] **Amy:** but then if they don't they're shunned so it's a little different

[8:51:30 a.m.] **Amy:** haha

[8:51:41 a.m.] **Dave:** I won't shun you.

[8:51:45 a.m.] **Dave:** :)

[8:51:48 a.m.] **Amy:** thanks haha

[8:51:57 a.m.] **Amy:** but i think it's an interesting concept

[8:52:09 a.m.] **Dave:** very.

[8:52:26 a.m.] **Dave:** so are you thinking about checking out an Amish church?

[8:52:38 a.m.] **Amy:** no

[8:52:46 a.m.] **Amy:** how did you get that?

[8:52:52 a.m.] **Amy:** are you being funny?

[8:53:29 a.m.] **Dave:** you said, "I love the Amish"

[8:53:39 a.m.] **Dave:** not trying to be funny . . . but I was funny.

[8:54:06 a.m.] **Amy:** not i want to be amish

[8:54:16 a.m.] **Amy:** im saying i had a metaphorical rumspringa

[8:54:22 a.m.] **Amy:** and i freaking love technology

[8:54:26 a.m.] **Amy:** why would i give that up?

[8:54:33 a.m.] **Dave:** technology—me too!

[8:55:45 a.m.] **Dave:** is there a church that you are thinking about checking out?

[8:55:58 a.m.] **Amy:** megan found one she wants to go to

[8:56:26 a.m.] **Dave:** cool.

[8:57:05 a.m.] **Amy:** i feel like i've separated myself so much that i could actually go in without all the pressure

[8:57:17 a.m.] **Amy:** and that no one knows me so i could be as into it as i want

[8:57:33 a.m.] **Amy:** i don't have to buy into everything right away

[8:58:38 a.m.] **Dave:** true.

[8:58:51 a.m.] **Dave:** it puts you in a good place to be you.

[8:59:25 a.m.] **Amy:** which is what im best at

[8:59:30 a.m.] **Amy:** if i say so myself

[8:59:33 a.m.] **Dave:** well said!

[8:59:48 a.m.] **Amy:** this is starting to feel very disney channel

[8:59:50 a.m.] **Dave:** YOU are a brilliant YOU!

[9:00:02 a.m.] **Dave:** (fade in music)

[9:00:27 a.m.] **Amy:** (and impromptu dance number)

[9:00:47 a.m.] **Dave:** (crescendo . . . and go to black)

[9:01:21 a.m.] **Amy:** are you in a meeting right now?

[9:01:27 a.m.] **Dave:** yes.

[9:01:40 a.m.] **Amy:** haha

[10:03:36 a.m.] **Dave:** "rumspringa" I'm going to keep thinking about that. Great word.

[10:10:34 a.m.] **Amy:** mhmmm it's german

[10:47:56 a.m.] **Dave:** gotta go . . . I LOVE YOU!!

HE STARTS WALKING

Rumspringa—it's what the prodigal son did. It's what we all do before we find our way back to God. Like the younger son, we reject the things of the Father and set out on our own. We search for a love more satisfying than his. We pursue causes that are not directed by him. We try to make sense out of life without a loving God in the equation. We get ourselves lost in God's big world, and when we are ready we come back to him, and he refuses to hold it against us.

This is the hinge in what might be the most important story Jesus ever told. The young man comes to his senses. And then he acts. He picks himself up. He turns from all that took him away from his father. And he starts walking toward home. Rumspringa is past. Repentance is here. He is ready to start over.

How about you? Are you ready to start over? If you'll stay with me on this journey, I will introduce you to the help you need to find your way home.

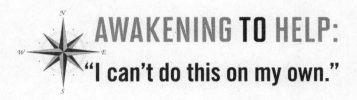

AWAKENING TO HELP:
"I can't do this on my own."

He got up and went to his father.
—Luke 15:20

9

I Want to Come Home

If the lost son needed a theme song for this third awakening, the Beatles could answer the call with their song "Help!"

Help, I need somebody.
Help, not just anybody.

Part story, part confession, the hit song expresses one of the primal cries of the human race. In the song, a young man has awakened to a need he didn't think he'd ever experience. He needs help! Sure, he used to brag he could do it alone, but that was pride and ignorance talking, and those days are gone. Today he feels shaken, alone, about to crash and burn. He's opening up the doors, and he's crying out, "Help!"

And the rest of us sing along at the top of our lungs, 'cause we know the feeling exactly!

Now back to Jesus's story. When the lost son came to his senses, he made a decision he never expected to make. "Here I am starving to death, and everyone back home has plenty to eat!" he groaned. "I want to go home . . . and I will."[53] He was ready to stop trying to do life by himself, on his own terms.

We don't hear him yelling to be rescued, but we see it in his words and his actions. He is crying out for help.

Jon and I call this major leap forward in our journey back to God the *awakening to help*. It's the next step beyond the awakening to regret—that's where we started to feel the full heaviness of the bad that we've done or the bad that's been done to us and wanted with all our hearts to start over. This third awakening moves us a giant step closer to God because we choose change at almost any cost, and we realize we can't do it alone. What happens next?

We make a call.

We have that conversation.

We walk into a support group.

We find ourselves sliding into the back row at church—no one more surprised than us.

We fall on our knees and cry out, "God, if you're real . . . !"

In the case of the lost son, he faced the truth and made a decision. Here are the lines from the story where the son is talking to himself:

"I will set out and go back to my father and say to him: Father, I have sinned against heaven and against you. I am no longer worthy to be called your son; make me like one of your hired servants." So he got up and went to his father.[54]

You have to wonder what he imagined his reception would be. He can't show up at the house as if nothing's happened, can he? You don't do what he did and then come traipsing back, saying, "Hey, Dad! I'm home! What's for dinner?"

But his confession shows that he knows what he's done and that he has to make it right—or at least try to. It's a crucial step for anyone on a journey back to God.

He repents.

TESHUVAH

In the previous chapter, we talked about repentance as doing a one-eighty. We said that repentance is the realization that the direction we are headed in is taking us far from God and all the good he wants for us. And so we *turn from* what we were pursuing and *turn toward* God. That's *metanoia,* a Greek word from the New Testament.

But the Bible was written in two languages. Let's take a closer look at what the Old Testament word for "repent" means. It gives us a crucial nuance.

The Hebrew word for repent is *teshuvah,* and it is maybe even more interesting than metanoia, at least for those of us on a spiritual journey. Teshuvah means "to go back to where you belong." For the son in the story, that meant to go back home to his father.

So when we read that the lost son "got up and went to his father," we realize that this is the turning point in his story. This is where he knows he needs help and he can't do this on his own. He is on his way home. Back to where he belongs.

And that is the outcome of repenting for any of us.

We go home.

Home—what a great word, huh? I don't know if there's another word in the English language quite like the word *home* when it comes to what it means to most people. It brings to mind all sorts of heartwarming thoughts and phrases: "Let's go home." "Welcome home." "There's no place like home." "Just wait till your father gets home." (Okay, so that last one is not so good.) If we didn't grow up in a healthy, loving home, the pain that the word *home* conjures up reflects our longing for what we didn't have growing up.

To repent is to go home, returning to where you came from and where you belong. Finding your way back to God is not a temporary quick fix. This is not about going home, resting up for a while, getting your clothes laundered, and eating a hot meal before wandering away again. Going home is about being forgiven and receiving assurance of life after this life, but it's also about finding new meaning and direction for life that you can't find anywhere else.

God provides incredible blessings to anyone who comes to him. But going home to him isn't only about wanting what God can do for you. It's about having a relationship with God. It's about redirecting your life and returning to where you've come from and where you belong. When you repent and go home, God changes you. You are different. The Bible says that God's Spirit comes to live inside you, and that results in a recognizable and ongoing transformation.

Dallas Willard, a philosopher and author, gave a definition I love. He said that *repent* means to "change the way you've been thinking and acting."[55]

A CHANGE OF DIRECTION

This April, Jon and his wife, Lisa, will celebrate another wedding anniversary. Jon says, "There are few choices in my life that required a change of direction like getting married. I had to reconfigure my strategy for living. For example, I had to reconfigure my strategy for laundry. No longer could I leave my socks on the floor with no regard. And I had to reconfigure my strategy for the kitchen. No longer could I let the dirty dishes pile up to the point where it required a front-end loader to put them in the dishwasher. I had to reconfigure my strategy for the bathroom. No longer could I leave the toilet seat up with no concern for someone else's late-night trips to the bathroom."

Truth is, any relationship worth pursuing requires you to reconfigure your strategy for living.

We all need turnaround strategies at some point. We have plans for how we'll change our lives or deal with pain from the past or escape stress from the present. Sometimes we pull it off—things change for the better, and we're glad we've moved on. But too often our plans to change direction include the word *over:* overeating, overdrinking, overspending, overexercising, or "oversexing."

We end up reconfiguring things, all right, but not for the better.

I don't mention these strategies so any of us will feel bad, because repentance doesn't mean feeling bad. As a matter of fact, Scripture says true repentance leads to times of refreshing from the Lord.[56] Remember, repentance is about starting over and admitting, "I need help."

This call to repent, to turn away from our sin and return home to God, is for everyone. No matter where we may be on our journey of finding our way back to God, we all have stuff in our lives that we are still holding on to. For some, it's a secret activity or habit that nobody else knows about. For others, it's pretty obvious what we're still chasing.

What is it for you? What are you still chasing, hoping it will somehow finally satisfy?

What do you need to let go of? Jon and I can tell you from personal experience that God rarely puts something new in your life until you let go of something old and broken.

We are all prodigals who have left home and turned away from our heavenly Father. Our Father is calling us to come home to the One who brought us into existence out of love, to come home to the eternal community where we belong, and to come home to the only One who loves us so much that he would rather die than live without us.

This could be the day you go home. God wants you to do what the lost son did. Get up from where you are and come home to where you belong. It does not matter what poor decisions you have made in the past. He's saying to you, "Whatever you have done, whatever you have become, it doesn't matter. Just come home."

When I think of people who have learned the lesson about needing help and coming home to God, my mind immediately goes to my friend Steve.

RESIGNING GODHOOD

For a long time, Steve thought he had no need to find his way back to God. Why? Because he thought he *was* God. At least he thought he had control of his life and could do anything he wanted to.

Steve is a bright guy who discovered early on that he had a gift for entrepreneurship. Not long after graduating college, he was already making a lot of money through the business he started. Soon he married a beautiful woman, bought a big house with her, and started a family.

At the same time, though, he was living a destructive, secret life. He thought he could keep things from his wife. He thought he could hold his two lives together. But it began to wear on him. All the time, he was living with guilt and the fear of what would happen if his vices were found out.

Steve had grown up going to church, but he had lost interest in God at an early age. Now, though, he started sensing that he needed something spiritual in his life again. But there was an obstacle standing in the way: himself.

Looking back on this time, Steve says, "I was having a yearning to find this thing called God, but I was so self-willed, so stubborn that I thought I was God. I'd thrown away all my religion. I didn't want to submit to anything else."

Then a golfing buddy invited him to join a group of men who got together weekly to talk about their lives and relate their personal issues to the Bible. Steve said sure he'd come. He went into that men's group ready to teach the other men about all the ways they were wrong.

But it was Steve who learned instead.

It took almost two years of that men's group showing Steve week after week what God meant to them before it finally started to sink in. Steve couldn't believe that, no matter what sins and stories he shared with the guys, they were never judgmental. In fact, they praised him for his honesty instead. Steve had finally experienced this thing called *grace,* and it blew him away. One day Steve got down on his knees with the leader of the group and prayed for the saving and healing grace of Jesus.

Steve recalls, "When I asked Jesus to come into my life, he did. He lifted me up and convicted me both." It was the start of living for God and not for himself, of living a life he didn't have to hide.

But even with these changes, God did not "fix" everything in Steve's life. In fact, life got harder for him. Shortly after becoming a Christ follower, Steve watched both his parents pass away. Then all the damage he had done for so many years resulted in divorce and a painful and humiliating custody battle over his kids. Right about then, Steve was diagnosed with cancer and given less than a year to live.

While the Christ-following life hasn't been anywhere close to easy for Steve, that hasn't caused him to lose faith. He explains, "Christ has helped me through every one of those challenges. So the question for me isn't 'What is God doing for me?' The question is 'What is he *not* doing for me?'"

Today Steve has partial custody of his kids and has survived cancer longer than the doctors predicted. He knows that more change and more challenges await him on his continuing spiritual journey with God. But there's no other journey he'd rather be on. Once he gave up being "god," the real God welcomed him with open arms.

Isn't that what you want? To repent—to reconsider and reconfigure your strategy for living? To teshuvah—to go back home?

Let's be honest, though. When we've been out there hurting ourselves and others with our foolish, self-centered decisions, it's hard to believe that a warm and welcoming embrace is waiting for us back home.

But what if it is?

Philip Yancey, author and communicator, spoke at a retreat where I was present and told the following modern-day version of the lost son's story.

WELCOME HOME, CHRISTA!

Her name was Christa, and she grew up on a small cherry farm in Traverse City, Michigan. She was a wild child who dismissed her parents as old-fashioned because of how they responded to her piercings and tattoos. One night Christa and her parents had a huge fight. At the end of it, she slammed the door and said, "I hate you," then acted on a plan she had been rehearsing for months in her mind. She ran away to the big city of Detroit.

Within a few hours of arriving in Detroit, she met a man who seemed warm and nice. He drove the most expensive car she'd ever seen, and he was willing to take her in. This nice man taught her a few things that would make her valuable on the streets, and because Christa was young, she brought in top dollar for her services. As time went on, and as she got a little older, she wasn't bringing in top dollar anymore, and so she was thrown out on the street, with no money and a drug habit to support.

One night she thought back to those sunny spring days when she would be lying beneath the cherry trees. Realizing that renting her body on the streets of Detroit was no way to live, she decided she would head north, maybe move to Canada and start over. On her way north, she figured she'd try something that she thought had no chance of actually working. She mustered up enough courage to give her parents a call. No one answered, but she left a message telling them she was going to be passing through Traverse City on her way to Canada. If they wanted to see her, she would be at the bus station around midnight. After hanging up, she thought leaving the message was a stupid thing to do because odds were they were happier now that she was gone.

As the bus headed north, she could see the signs saying the bus was getting closer to Traverse City. She ran through the possible scenarios in her mind: nobody there to meet her; someone there, but only to shame her and condemn her. Finally the bus arrived in Traverse City, and she heard the bus driver say, "Fifteen minutes at this stop, fifteen minutes."

All her mental rehearsing didn't prepare her for what she found when she stepped off the bus. At midnight in this small-town bus depot, she found dozens of familiar faces belonging to aunts, uncles, cousins, and grandparents, all wearing silly party hats. A huge banner hanging from the walls said, "WELCOME HOME, CHRISTA!!!" Her dad broke through the crowd and ran up to her, and as she tried to explain herself, he wrapped his arms around her, making it clear that all he really cared about was that his daughter was home.[57]

DISCOVERING A DIFFERENT FATHER

Are you ready to take the next step toward your heavenly Father? The third awakening on your journey of finding your way back to God happens when you admit, "I need help." For most of us, that realization is hard earned. It might even fill us with fear, especially if we think of God as the angry judge, ready to make us pay for every single mistake we've made. Who wants to come home to that?

But in the next chapter, you're going to discover a very different Father— a Father you may never have thought existed. You're going to discover, for example, that your cry for help has already been heard. That your Father is already hurrying in your direction.

Do you believe me?

It's time to put this God to the test. Simply say this prayer:

> God, if you are real,
> make yourself real to me.
> Awaken in me the willingness
> to turn toward you for help.

10

The God Who Runs

As the lost son heads for home, he has to be thinking about what his father's reaction to him will be. Will he get the door slammed in his face? Will he have to endure an almighty chewing-out and *then* get the door slammed in his face? Will he be given the servant's job he is planning to beg for—but only at the cost of constant reminders of how he forfeited his status in the family?

The young man doesn't know how his father will respond. He knows he has blown it big time and humiliated his dad in the worst possible way. He must be preparing for rejection.

But look what happened next in Jesus's story:

While he was still a long way off, his father saw him and was filled with compassion for him; he ran to his son, threw his arms around him and kissed him.[58]

What a surprising turn of events! From despair, starvation, and dread to the warmest homecoming scene ever!

In the next awakening, we'll be focusing on God's love and what it means for a returning child of God. But before we even get to that, we need to recognize the welcoming nature of God. When we realize that we are inadequate to start our life over again on our own, we can have the courage to seek God's help because he is waiting to receive us. That's the kind of God he is. And his loving nature should cause us to be willing to take a chance on him.

In this light, don't miss the moment when the father in Jesus's story first sets his eyes on the son walking nervously up the road. The story says, "While he was still a long way off, his father saw him."

Read those words again. What does that tell you about the father? What is so significant about the fact that the father saw his son while he was still a long way off? The father had no reason to expect his son to return anytime soon. The son didn't text him or phone him in advance to let him know he was coming.

How long had he been gone? Weeks? Months? Years? His father had many important matters to attend to. Why was he scanning the horizon hoping to catch a glimpse of his son returning home? His friends had to be telling him, "Forget about that worthless son of yours. Look what he did to you. He's getting what he deserves. Go on with your life." People likely encouraged him to move on. But he wouldn't move on.

Scandalous Grace

The picture I have in my mind is the father out on his front porch every day, looking into the distance, his heart aching, wanting more than anything else to see his son again.

Finally, on this occasion, after who knows how long a period of disappointment, he sees a figure in the distance. Maybe he thinks his eyes are playing tricks on him. But no, this is real. It is his son! And when he sees him, he takes off in a sprint.

The son, who is prepared to clear whatever bar his father sets, high or low, finds when he gets home that there is no bar. No lectures. No standoffishness. No need for promises of doing better. No need to grovel or prove his sincerity. Just open arms and tears of joy and celebration.

The son has done the unthinkable, rejected the most important relationship in his life, and he doesn't have to do anything to be forgiven; he just has to come home. This is what we call grace. You may have heard about God's grace, but do you grasp it?

It's surprising.

It's astonishing.

It's spectacular.

It's moving.

It's incomprehensible.

It's amazing.

It's even scandalous.

Even now, you may be asking some clarifying questions: *Is there really no bar to clear to be reconciled to my heavenly Father? Are you suggesting that the only relationship in this life that will determine a person's eternity is not based on clearing a bar of worthiness or getting my act together even just a little? Is it true that the fundamentalist God with the bar set high is not real and that the liberal God with the bar set low is not real either? Do you mean that there is no bar to clear at all? How is that possible?*

Well, actually, there is a bar. Just one. And Jesus hung from it. Finding your way back to God is not about what you do — it is about what Jesus already did.

With his story, Jesus paints a mind-boggling picture of a God who is over the top with grace and mercy and love for anyone who wants to come home to him. It's the main point of the story. Jesus is saying, "When you've blown it and admit, 'I need help,' and you come home to your heavenly Father, this is how God responds to you. That's the kind of reception you can expect from him."

WHAT DO YOU BELIEVE ABOUT GOD?

The key question is this: Do you believe that the story Jesus told paints a true picture of God?

Don't answer that question too quickly.

First I want you to think about God's grace in a certain way. Bear with me if this feels a little over the top, okay? Are you ready?

Let's say your number was up today. Your life is over; it is time to face God personally and give an account of your life. It is time for God to declare whether you will be with him forever in heaven or be separated from him. In that moment, God welcomes you just as the father welcomed the prodigal.

What's your reaction to God's grace? I think the responses people have to that question tend to sort themselves into three major groups. Think about the options and decide which group you belong to.

Group 1—"I Don't Believe It."

I know many people who believe in God with their heads but not with their hearts. When I talk to them, I sometimes sense them thinking, *He may welcome* you *with open arms, but not* me. *You don't know all the stuff I've done.*

The lost son had to be thinking something like that on his way home: What's the use? I've messed up so badly, I've gone so far and disrespected my dad so much, there is no way he is going to take me back, no matter what I say or do.

We tend to rate our actions on some kind of sin-o-meter, don't we? We categorize some sins as particularly bad—the ones that hurt others, such as sexual sin or violence toward someone. We think, *The lost-son story is a nice one, but I would never expect God to forgive me, let alone be glad to see me.* You may feel this way because of personal failures and a sense of shame over something you've done or something that was done to you. People sometimes say, "When I face God, I don't expect a warm welcome. In fact, I expect the opposite."

There are times I struggle with this myself. I know in my head that God loves me, even unconditionally. I take him for his word on that. But sometimes I all but ignore him and go consecutive days without spending any significant time with him in prayer. On too many occasions, I give in to temptation that I know saddens him, whether it's a lack of sensitivity to the people I care about most or a pursuit of acceptance and popularity at the expense of integrity. It's when I do some of the same stupid stuff over and over again that I find the distance from my head to my heart increasing, and the reality of his grace becomes a fading memory.

How about you? Down deep, do you expect God to run toward you and shower you with affection? Or would you have to say, "No, deep down that's not what I expect"?

Group 2—"I Expect It!"

A second group might say, "God is a God of love and forgiveness, and though I'm not perfect, I'm no ax murderer or terrorist. So sure, if I had to face God, I would expect a warm welcome. Forgiveness is God's business; it's just what he does."

When Jesus told this story of the lost son, among his listeners were Pharisees. They were the professional religious guys who were considered to be the spiritual elite. They would have been the ones who would have said they expected that kind of welcome from God. They would never have claimed to be perfect. They would have claimed to be good enough.

It has been centuries since any religious group referred to itself as Pharisees. The term is now associated with being self-righteous and hypocritical. However, before we assume we would never belong in this second group, let's examine our thinking. I wonder if this attitude toward God creeps into our mind-set so subtly that we hardly notice it. Maybe you once were blown away by the extravagance of God's grace, but over the years it has lost its impact. Perhaps there was a time when you sang, "Amazing grace how sweet the sound that saved a wretch like me," and the words brought tears to your eyes and deep thankfulness to your heart. But now it all feels a little too routine, maybe a little old hat. The shock and awe of God's love and grace has been replaced by a simple assent: "I'm all good because God is a God of grace and love. He'll give me a pass. That's what I expect from God."

Take another look at this story. Jesus describes a son who got the opposite of what he expected. The father was anxiously waiting and watching for his son to come home. He couldn't wait for him to arrive, and when he did, the father was so overjoyed that he ran out to hug him and kiss him. Then he threw an extravagant party in his honor. That is a far cry from what the person who considers himself to be "good enough" is expecting from God.

"HE RAN"

Put yourself in the place of the lost son on his way home. He's desperate, starving, making the long trek back to his hometown crushed by his mistakes. He knows what's coming. He expects to face hostility and humiliation from everybody in town. What he had done—squandering his inheritance and birthright—was a disgrace.

Jesus says the father saw the son "and was filled with compassion for him."[59] The father wasn't filled with indignation. He wasn't filled with anger. He wasn't filled with retribution. He was filled with *compassion.*

Then what follow are some of the most incredible words in all of Scripture. Jesus says this about the father:

He ran to his son.

Important men don't run. Have you ever seen the president of the United States or the CEO of a major corporation run to greet someone? Important people walk. Running is undignified. Running is inappropriate. This was especially true in Jesus's culture. The father, the patriarch, the head of the family would never act in such an improper manner.

But the lost son's father ran.

There are no words that could fully capture what happens next. This father sees his son. He sees the baby that he held so carefully in his arms. He's reminded of the toddler who took his first steps. He remembers the boy he prayed over and the young man he feared he would never see again. Now this boy is before him, so withered that he's not much more than skin and bones. The father throws his arms around his son whom he thought was lost for good, and he refuses to let go. It's an embrace that neither the father nor son will ever forget.

Then he kisses his son. The way Jesus describes this father kissing his son means that he kisses him repeatedly, again and again. He can't stop. The father says nothing because his hugs and kisses say more than words could possibly communicate.

Finally the son speaks.

Father, I have sinned against heaven and against you. I am
no longer worthy to be called your son.[60]

Did you catch that? He anticipated the possibility of public ridicule. He wondered if his father would banish him from home forever, and he knew he deserved it. I believe he thought through every imaginable scenario, but I doubt he ever expected what he received. He was prepared to be run out of town, but not to have his dad run out to welcome him and throw a party in his honor.

Until you come to the place where you don't really expect to be accepted unconditionally and extravagantly by the Father, you won't understand what Jesus is revealing here. Thinking you grade high enough on the sin curve is a far cry from the prodigal's willingness to face up to the truth—no excuses.

What I'm about to say next may bother you.

To expect God to welcome you home because of what you have or haven't done, or because you consider yourself a decent person, is to totally misunderstand the grace of God. Actually, it is tragically arrogant, because you are not seeing the truth of who you are.

Who you are (if you haven't already seen it) is the lost son in the story. Which, in a surprising way, is actually good news. You see, only when we grasp the truth that each of us *is* the lost son can we know the joy that comes from experiencing our Father's extravagant grace.

I am a lost son. More days than I care to admit, I am selfish and self-absorbed. In one way or another, I rebel—I run away from home—squandering incredible blessing from my heavenly Father. I wake up too many mornings and live too many days ungrateful, uncaring, and unconcerned about what matters to God. I'm amazed that he still keeps calling me home and wants nothing more than for me to come back to him so he can run to me and wrap me in his strong embrace.

Is it hard for me to believe that God feels that way about me? Sure is. But do I believe it? Yes. Because of what Jesus shows us in his story.

When Jesus shows us a Father who watches for us, comes running toward us with compassion, and wraps us in a huge hug, he is showing us the heart of God. This Father's heart is so full that he is looking for people upon whom he can pour his extravagant grace. It's not for people who are stuck on being good enough or not good enough. It's for people who know they need help. They are lost sons and daughters who want to come home. And because of who he is, God comes to their aid.

IT'S WHAT A GOOD DAD DOES

Derek Redmond may be the most famous Olympian to ever finish last. In 1992 at the Barcelona Olympics, the British sprinter was almost halfway to the finish line in the four-hundred-meter semifinal race when he felt the pain that would mark the end of his sprinting career and, as reporter Kurt Wagner wrote, the "beginning of one of history's most unforgettable Olympic moments."

Redmond was running well, confident that he would finish first in the event, when suddenly his hamstring tore. The excruciating pain forced him to the ground, but he was determined to finish. He half hopped and half ran down the track. "The thought that went through my mind, as crazy as it sounds now, was 'I can still catch them,'" recalled Redmond. "I just remember thinking to myself, 'I'm not going to stop. I'm going to finish this race.'"

Jim Redmond, Derek's father, watched from the stands as his son struggled around the final turn. Wagner described what happened next as "one of the most powerful images in Olympic history." Jim Redmond broke through security, ran to his hurting son, put his arm around him, and helped Derek finish the final seventy-five meters of the race. The pair crossed the finish line to one of the largest ovations in Olympic history.[61]

You have a Father who will run to be with you in the middle of your greatest failure and your deepest pain. While your biggest disappointment and greatest hurts will leave you humbled and in tears, he will come alongside you. It's what a father does. Grace. For our God, it's instinctive. When shame reminds you of your greatest defeats, he will be there to remind you, "You are my child. I could never love you more, and I will never love you less. Whatever you've done, you are forgiven. You are always and unconditionally loved."

Crazy, isn't it? If you would *never* expect it but you *can* believe it, you are a part of the final group.

Group 3—"I Don't Expect It, but I Believe It!"

Those in the third group believe that God is all Jesus says he is—the father of the lost son. And they believe it because they know the One who told this story.

So important is this third way of looking at the situation that we'll spend the whole next chapter considering it.

11

Help Has a Name

Let's step back from the story Jesus told to look more closely at the Storyteller himself. It's time to consider the Author more closely because—don't miss this!—he is the key to understanding what the story means to you.

The novelist Charles Dickens was fascinated by the theme of atonement (more on that later). It's often said that he called the parable of the lost son "the greatest short story ever told." Many others would agree with him.

Why? I'm going to go out on a limb and say that the reason the lost son's story is such a wonderfully powerful parable is because it's your story, it's my story, it's everyone's story. We all find ourselves far from where we thought we would be. And the author, Jesus, is the preeminent authority on how to find your way.

Need help finding God?

Help has a name. Jesus.

WHO *WAS* HE, ANYWAY?

My friend Aaron is a Jewish man who grew up in Boston with parents who were atheists. He spent more than the first four decades of his life believing the notion of God to be one of the most absurd concepts he had ever heard. He had no need for God. He had all he needed in his beautiful wife, three wonderful children, lucrative career as a psychologist, good friends, and all the toys he wanted.

One day Aaron found himself in a conversation with a close friend who asked him what he thought of Jesus. Aaron responded the way he always did in this kind of situation: "He was a great teacher, a great prophet, and a heck of a carpenter!"

The friend went on to explain that he believed Jesus was God.

Aaron rolled his eyes and said something disparaging about his friend's willingness to believe foolish notions.

His friend said the notion of Jesus being God wasn't just something others have said about Jesus. It was something Jesus said about himself. Then he challenged Aaron: "If this was not true, and Jesus lied about being God, how could you or anyone else consider him to be a great anything?"

The logic in that hit Aaron hard. He said to himself, *If the claims Jesus made about himself being God are not true, then that makes him the worst kind of person to ever walk the earth. But if his claims about being God are true . . .*

Aaron proceeded to read a book that his friend gave him suggesting that there are only three possibilities for the claims Jesus made: he was either a complete liar, totally insane, or exactly who he claimed to be—God.

My friend knew he couldn't make a reasonable argument for either of the first two options. Aaron told me, "First, no human being could lie to the extent Jesus did. Why would he go through all he went through for a lie? All he had to do was shut up. And if it was a lie, it was the dumbest lie ever. People are willing to lie for something self-serving, but there was nothing really in this for Jesus, and for it he died.

"Second, Jesus was far too consistent to be crazy. I'm in the mental health industry, and crazy people are not linear or consistent. Jesus was consistent, always loving, always kind, and always generous."

Aaron then said he came to a page in the book where he read the question that would change his life: "Do you now realize that there is only one option left?"[62] The concept that Jesus was exactly who he said he was did not merely strike Aaron's brain as true. It struck his heart as true. Aaron had found his way back to God through Jesus.

We could say he now belonged to group 3—people who don't expect God's grace but believe it is for them anyway. Why the change? Because he now knew the Storyteller.

Friend, the most important step in our awakening to help is to meet the Narrator of our story. Not just to learn about our need for help or to know about God from the story, but to meet the Storyteller.

And here's the reason: Jesus's sole intent for telling this story was to help us find our way back to God. The reason he knows so much about finding God is because he *is* God. Not some remote God who is "out there" and doesn't really care about what's going on in our lives, but a God who is present and active. A relational God who is seeking you at the same time you are seeking him.

JESUS: GOD *WITH* US

An angel prophesied about Jesus's birth,

> *The virgin will conceive and give birth to a son, and they will call*
> *him Immanuel (which means "God with us").*[63]

The One who told the story of how to get back to God was sent by God to us. He came and lived with us and was one of us—fully God and fully human.

In 1961 the Soviet Union put the first man into space. Nikita Khrushchev was premier of the Soviet Union at the time and an outspoken advocate of atheism. In a speech he gave after the first cosmonaut went into space, Khrushchev said, "Gagarin flew in space and saw no God."[64]

C. S. Lewis, considered one of the great minds of the twentieth century, wrote a response. He said that if there is a God, you would relate to him in the way Hamlet would relate to Shakespeare. Hamlet could not find Shakespeare by going backstage or looking up in the rafters. The only way Hamlet could discover anything about Shakespeare would be if Shakespeare wrote himself into the play.[65]

The Author of the lost-son story wrote himself into history by coming to earth to live among us and do life with us. For all of history, people have wondered and speculated and debated about what God is really like, but in Jesus, God became part of history and our story so that God can be known. Immanuel. God with us. This is unique to Jesus. And it is the reason he is findable, if we are yearning to come back to God.

But there's still more to Jesus's divine nature that makes it possible for us to connect with him.

JESUS: GOD *FOR* US

The Author of the lost-son story did more than come to earth to be with us; Jesus also proved his love for us. Since the first century, people have recognized this truth about Jesus:

> *Being found in appearance as a man,*
> *he humbled himself*
> *by becoming obedient to death—*
> *even death on a cross!*[66]

Jesus made the decision that he would rather die than live without us.

This is perfectly illustrated in Charles Dickens's classic *A Tale of Two Cities*. Whether you actually read the book or just resorted to the CliffsNotes back in tenth grade, you probably know it as an incredible story. The two main characters are Charles Darnay and Sydney Carton, and they look very similar. They also happen to love the same person, a woman named Lucy. The beautiful Lucy ends up choosing Darnay, and they marry and have a child.

The setting for the story is the French Revolution. Darnay is rounded up, imprisoned in the Bastille, and sentenced to die. So Sydney Carton and a few companions sneak into the jail cell, and Carton suggests he and Darnay switch clothes so Carton will be mistaken for Darnay. Then Darnay will be free to live the rest of his life with Lucy and their child.

Darnay refuses and says he would never allow him to do such a thing. So Carton does what any good friend would do—he drugs him to knock him out. Carton is then carted off and Darnay is set free.

But as Carton awaits his execution, another prisoner, thinking Carton is Darnay, comes to speak with him. She is terrified about her death, and as she talks to him, she begins to realize that the switch has been made. She asks Carton, "Are you dying for him?"

"And his wife and child. Hush! Yes."

"O, you will let me hold your brave hand, stranger?"[67]

She was so moved by Carton's willingness to die for another that she found the courage to face her own death.

Carton's sacrifice is a lot like what Jesus did for us. He died taking our place. He is a God who is for us. Theologians call his actions for us on the cross the *atonement*. Atonement is making reparation for wrongs and reconciling us to God. We couldn't do that on our own. We needed help. And Jesus stepped in and died for us. He offered us the help we need.

"I WILL BE FOUND BY YOU"

The reason I can, with great confidence, ask you to make a wager in prayer on God's being real is because I know the Author of the story. He is the same one who told us, "I will be found by you."[68]

If you have been praying, "God, if you are real, make yourself real to me," you have probably felt his presence in ways you can't explain. You might have experienced situations that are far more than coincidences. It is God pursuing you. Or maybe you have noticed an awareness or energy in your life that wasn't there before. It's God! What God wants is you. A relationship with you.

My friend Tony was raised in a Christian home, but he just went through the motions of going to church services and, as he says, "doing what Christians do." As soon as he went off to college, he stopped all the pretending and took a long walk on the wild side.

After Tony graduated, he moved to another part of the world and got involved in all kinds of messed-up stuff. His family pleaded with him to come back to God, but he flatly said, "Nope, that's for you and not for me. This is how I want to live."

Then one day, after nearly ten years of running from God, he was playing basketball when he blew out his knee. Doctors told him that he needed a specialist and had to return to the United States to have reconstructive surgery. He would need to find a place to live for at least three months so he could rehab his knee. He knew he needed help, and he had nowhere to go other than home to his parents. So Tony went to live at his mom and dad's place.

His parents hosted a small-group Bible study in their home, and in this small group was a young woman whom Tony had his eye on. He'd had more sexual partners than he could remember, including plenty who claimed to be committed Christians, so he was sure he could get this girl into bed. He started going to this small group, expecting to reel her in.

What he didn't expect was how this group took him in. This girl invited him to church. He went, and he started hearing about Jesus in a way that was different from anything he'd ever heard before. Something inside him began to change. Tony turned his life around, decided to follow Jesus, and acknowledged it by being baptized.

He came home to get a reconstructed knee but ended up with a reconstructed relationship with God. As he looks back on that experience, he says, "When God is pursuing you, he doesn't mess around." God wouldn't give up on Tony, even though Tony had given up on God.

In Jesus, God came to earth in pursuit of all of us. God "doesn't want anyone lost."[69] Maybe this is the moment for you to be found.

The Way Back to God

It's interesting that Jesus isn't the only author who told a story with a prodigal son in it. Another major world religion has a story with a prodigal son too. The story has roughly the same characters. It has a similar setting. The plot unfolds in the same way. And the inner conflict of the younger son is identical. But the stories diverge at the point of resolution—when the father finds the son, the father makes him live in poverty for twenty years so he can learn the error of his ways.

That storyteller does not know God.

Jesus says, "I am the way and the truth and the life."[70] He is reminding us that he *does* know God, that he *is* God, and that, if we follow him, he is the way back to new life in God.

Like Aaron, you have only three choices: Jesus is a liar, a lunatic, or the Lord. Which is it for you? If you respond with "Lord," then you are acknowledging that Jesus is the way back to God. You'll find your way by following Jesus.

"Follow me" were Jesus's simple words to his first two disciples, Peter and Andrew, offering them a zoe kind of life that would start at once and go on forever.[71] Jesus is giving you the same simple challenge: *Follow me.* If you follow Jesus in this life, you will follow him into the next. Jesus promised, "Whoever acknowledges me before others, I will also acknowledge before my Father in heaven."[72] If you will declare yourself a Christ follower right now, he will declare that he knows you in heaven forever.

Maybe this is old news for you. Maybe you began following Christ years ago. But somewhere along the way, you lost sight of him and wandered off the path. For any number of possible reasons, he seems distant to you. And you want to get back the closeness you once felt with him as he walked with you side by side. You can choose him again. You can decide to follow him . . . again. As many times as you fall away from him, you can repent, receive his grace, and start again. That's such a beautiful thing about Jesus: his boundless capacity to receive the spiritual returnees.

If you have been reading everything we've said about owning up to your deep need for help, and you have a deep desire to choose (or re-choose) Jesus as Lord of your life, you have awakened to your need for help. No, you can't start over in life and form a relationship with God all in your own power. You need grace from Jesus for that. But it's available, because Jesus is God and he is the way to God. And you are deciding to follow him.

Traveler, seeker, lost and loved child of God—welcome home!

On the other hand, if you say no to Jesus, then sadly, you'll never get beyond your stuckness and the regret in your life will only grow.

"I Miss Him"

You most likely know the name Billy Graham. But back in the late 1940s, just as many people knew the name Charles Templeton.

Templeton was a close friend and preaching associate of Billy Graham. He helped found an international Christian youth organization and built a large church in Toronto. But he came to a point in his life where his doubts got the better of him, and that doubt turned into disbelief, and he found himself an agnostic rejecting his Christian faith. He even said, "I feel sorry for Graham," explaining, "he committed intellectual suicide by closing his mind."[73] Templeton resigned from the ministry and wrote a critique of the Christian faith titled *Farewell to God: My Reasons for Rejecting the Christian Faith.*

A few years back, at the age of eighty-three, Templeton was interviewed about his life and spirituality. The interviewer asked him about Jesus and was surprised at the response. Templeton said this:

> He was . . . the greatest human being who has ever lived. He was a moral genius. His ethical sense was unique. He was the intrinsically wisest person that I've ever encountered in my life or in my readings. . . .
>
> He's the most important thing in my life. . . . I know it may sound strange, but I have to say . . . I adore *him!*
>
> Everything good I know, everything decent I know, everything pure I know, I learned from Jesus.
>
> He is the most important human being who has ever existed.

Then he added,

And if I may put it this way, I . . . miss . . . him![74]

And as he said it, his eyes filled with tears and he wept freely. He refused to say more.

The early theologian and philosopher Augustine said this about knowing God in Jesus: "You made us for yourself and our hearts find no peace until they rest in you."[75] Charles Templeton's heart remained uneasy at the end of his life because he resigned from following Jesus.

But if you believe the storyteller is God and you have begun to follow him, you have made a different choice—you have chosen not to live with that deep sense of missing God. It's as if you have walked through a gate and caught a glimpse of a whole new vista. You're seeing a place where your heart is at rest. You're home. How wonderful it is!

Being God's beloved child seems so great, in fact, that you may have a hard time convincing yourself it's even true.

AWAKENING **TO** LOVE:
"God loves me deeply after all."

Father, I have sinned against heaven
and against you. I am no longer
worthy to be called your son.
—Luke 15:21

12

The Shadow That Follows You Home

In the swirl of your new life with the Father, the next awakening may feel more like a step backward than a step forward. God is offering you something you want and need—a welcome home. But something inside you may want to resist. Jon and I have seen that reaction to grace show up in people's lives many times.

Resist is what the son in Jesus's story did. In that scene on the road, the father was single-minded in expressing his affection for his boy, his absolute delight that the son had returned. But the first words out of the prodigal's mouth were all about his terrible mistakes and letting the father know that he didn't feel like family anymore.

We've noted the son's rehearsed speech before. But now I want to point out that, even after seeing his father run to him, hug him, and kiss him—even after these unmistakable signs of the father's love and welcome—the son's opinion of himself couldn't immediately catch up with the new reality. He was still feeling unworthy of sonship.

The son said to him, "Father, I have sinned against heaven and against you. I am no longer worthy to be called your son."[76]

Your reflex may be similar. God's grace, acceptance, and forgiveness may strike you as just too much. Too good to be true, at least for you.

That feeling is understandable.

Get over it.

"WHATEVER YOU'VE DONE"

It was a small Texas town where everybody knew everything about everybody else. So when the Baptist pastor's son started dating the Church of Christ pastor's daughter, everybody thought it was a match made in heaven . . . until word got out that she was pregnant.

Two pastors' kids from two churches in a small Texas town who were not married and expecting a baby. In this conservative southern town, it could mean the end of both pastors' jobs and maybe the end of their ministries. This circumstance would be considered so shameful that it would follow these families and be talked about long after they were gone.

The son knew that he had to tell his dad himself, so he went home, and when he walked in the room to tell his dad about the pregnancy, he broke down crying. Amid the sobbing, he could only get out a few words: "I'm so sorry."

The father, not yet knowing what his son had done or why he was so upset, instinctively took a Bible off the shelf. He opened up the leather-bound book and started reading the story of the lost son and the father who welcomed him with open arms.

When the pastor finished reading the story, he wrapped his arms around his teenage son and said, "Whatever you've done—whatever it is—I want you to know I love you and you're forgiven. Nothing can change that. I could never love you more, and I will never love you less." With that, the father held him in his arms while his son wept.

I love that story because it parallels each of our stories. As we take steps back to God, we will be met by a heavenly Father who runs to embrace us and tell us, "Whatever you've done—whatever it is—you are forgiven and you are loved." Let that sink in. For you, it's ultimately and forever true.

"I Don't Deserve This"

Being welcomed home by your heavenly Father and received into the family—no questions asked—may seem totally unrealistic for someone who has wandered so far and so long.

You can see why we say that a spiritual tug of war accompanies our homecoming. We have one set of convictions about ourselves, and God has another. We look at our past filled with failure and shame, and he looks at who we are with love and compassion.

Jon and I are calling this stage of your journey your *awakening to love*. At this point, we start by saying, "I don't deserve this." His acceptance is just too unbelievable. But what God says and does is so entirely *opposite* what we think we deserve that we are moved to the most amazing realization: "God loves me deeply after all."

This awakening is a huge step forward, a breakthrough. We are realizing, perhaps for the first time, that none of us deserve a second chance, none of us deserve to be forgiven, and we certainly don't deserve to be loved unconditionally. But we are! *You* are! You don't deserve it, but God gives it to you anyway.

This grace is the most extravagant of gifts, and it's a gift that God gives freely to his children over and over again. But since Jon and I have discovered that lost kids newly returned home really struggle to hold on to the gift, we have another prayer wager that we want you to make. Simply say:

> God, if you are real,
> make yourself real to me.
> Awaken in me the awareness
> that I am your unconditionally loved child.

Keep saying it, because you're going to need a lot of confidence in God's grace to dispel the shadow of shame that has followed you home.

Let's go back to the lost (now found) son, because his example shows us the universal human tendency to lag behind the paradigm shift God's sudden grace brings to our world.

SHAME WHISPERS

We don't really understand how much reputation meant to people in Jesus's culture. Failures in that culture were never just individual; they reflected on a person's whole family. So the consequences of the son's bad choices meant unbearable embarrassment and shame not just for him but also for the father, the brother, and any other members of the family.

What is the son to make, then, of a dad who welcomes him back, holds him tight, and refuses to let go? The son can't help himself. He blurts out his self-judgment: "I am no longer worthy."

Don't you wonder how many times he had rehearsed those words on his long walk of shame? I bet he said it a thousand times!

I am no longer worthy . . .

I am no longer worthy . . .

I am no longer worthy . . .

But what if the son had allowed shame to keep him from coming home? What if he had allowed shame to keep him from accepting the father's love? How differently this story would have ended!

If you're like me, you know all about the soundtrack of shame. Shame whispers, "You don't really matter" and "You are not lovable." Shame shouts, "No more chances for you!" Shame brings self-condemnation, and when we first encounter grace, we find ourselves repeating, "I don't deserve this."

As a pastor trying to help many people in their spiritual journeys over the years, I've observed some things about shame. Let me make a point about shame, and see if it resonates in your experience.

It seems to me that shame shows up in our lives from two experiences. First, shame shows up when we do something wrong to someone else. When we lash out with anger, shame follows us with constant reminders of our behavior. When we are guilty of selfishness, it creeps back into our consciousness as guilt. When we let our base desires dictate our actions at the expense of others, shame accompanies us on our spiritual journey. It's just human—shame will follow us all the way back to our embrace with God and try to make it clear that we don't deserve it.

But shame's power still isn't exhausted. There are also times we are wronged by others in ways God never intended. When others abuse us, even if their guilt and our innocence are later exposed, shame lingers. When others don't love or value or respect us, shame sticks around long after they have left our lives. When we are the victims of the wrongdoing of others, shame deceives us with the same lie it uses when we are actually at fault. "You? You don't deserve this!"

Does any of this sound familiar?

Whatever the origin of the particular shame you are dealing with, there's something that has the power to force it out of your life.

THE EMBRACE OF GRACE

My mother-in-law, Lola, always seemed uncomfortable with hugging. She grew up in the home of an alcoholic where there was almost no expression of affection, tenderness, or love. Whenever I would greet her, I would extend my arms to hug her, but her response was always the same—an awkward three hard pats on the back and quick release. If you ask me, she just didn't feel safe in the embrace of another person.

Likewise, it's a struggle for many of us to feel comfortable in God's embrace. But in the middle of that struggle, he holds us tight and insists, "You are mine. I am yours. This is where you belong."

Maybe you have found yourself saying, "I don't deserve another chance," or "I don't deserve to be forgiven," or "I don't deserve grace." Listen, you are the very person Jesus told the lost-son story for. He wanted to pull you into the truth with a tale of grace you couldn't resist. He wanted you to reach for the unending forgiveness and unconditional love God has for you. Grace has the power to completely replace the guilt and shame in your life.

"You Can't Change Your Past, but God Can Change Your Future"

Shame held Leslie captive most of her life. She was ashamed of her dad, who was a compulsive gambler. She was ashamed of her mother, who had a string of affairs with married men during Leslie's growing-up years. She felt shame because of her own two divorces. She felt guilty when an ex-husband killed himself. Shame haunted her after the abortion she had when she was forty. Leslie said, "Shame was my prison, and it kept me hiding from the only One who could forgive me and set me free."

When Leslie courageously told her story for the first time, the light of grace began to filter into her darkness. As her friend listened closely to everything she had done and everything that had been done to her—those two sources of shame I identified earlier—she said, "Leslie, you can't change your past, but God can change your future." Those words were like a key unlocking her from a prison of shame and opening the door to a brand-new life.

Over the next several years, Leslie found her way back to God. She came to understand that her identity was not in what she had done or in what had been done to her. She says, "I am God's dearly loved child. Period."

At times she still thinks, *I don't deserve this.* But she also hears God's voice saying, "Whatever you've done, you are forgiven and you are loved." Today Leslie is helping other women who struggle with pain in their past to find their way back to God.

Do not let your past mistakes and failures define you. That is the voice of shame. You aren't what you've done or not done. You are not what's been done to you. You are who God says you are. His child.

WILL YOU DANCE?

Sophie grew up in a Christian home that valued discipline, excellence, and honor. So when she was young, her relationship with God could best have been described as formal and austere. She earnestly tried to honor God by memorizing Bible verses, praying, and going to church every time the church doors were open. She worked hard at being good.

But being good is different from being loved.

Although Sophie learned a lot about God beginning at an early age, he still felt so far away, so removed, so distant from her. She told me, "I had a faith in my head, but I didn't know God's heart and felt like he didn't know mine. I had heard a lot about God, but it wasn't until college that God began to woo me and I really found my way back to him."

She was at a college retreat to explore the life of Jesus. The speaker at the retreat asked Sophie and others to close their eyes. Sophie remembers thinking, *Oh great. Not one of those touchy-feely, close your eyes and visualize woo-woo things. I came here to study the Bible. I don't do that kind of stuff.* But since everyone was doing it, she joined in and closed her eyes. After a time of prayer and silence, the speaker said, "The time is now. God is here. How is God reaching out to you?"

Sophie describes that moment as "just a flash that hit my heart before my mind could take control. In that moment there was a mental picture that was like an ax to the frozen sea inside my heart."

Before I tell you what happened to her in that moment, I'll let Sophie take you back to an embarrassing experience she had when she was a schoolgirl. Here it is in her words:

When I was in junior high, I had to go to this awful program called Fortnightly. It was a manners and ballroom class that met, yes, fortnightly, every other Thursday. Think *Pride and Prejudice* for preteens. Girls had to wear dresses. Boys had to wear suits and ties. We were taught how to serve punch and do the fox trot and other ballroom dances.

Most of the time, we were assigned partners, but on Parents' Night they did things a little differently. With all the parents watching, girls were lined up against one wall of the dance floor, boys against the other. The teacher put on waltz music, and the boys were to cross the floor and choose a partner. The boys had to walk up to you, bow, and extend their hands. We were to curtsy and then take the boy's arm as we walked out to the middle of the floor. It was absolutely mortifying.

I remember standing in line, pleading to anyone and no one, *Please choose me. Please choose me. Please ask me to dance.* There was this mad scramble as boys rushed to the popular, pretty girls, and then there was this awkward hesitancy as the unlucky boys tried to decide among the rest of us. Soon it became clear that there was one more girl than boy. As the boys came toward us girls, I just knew. The other girls were asked to dance, and I hung my head and closed my eyes in shame.

When I looked up, I was standing against the wall alone. Utterly alone. I felt ugly, embarrassed, unwanted.

For Sophie, this experience on the dance floor was a perfect picture of how she felt about God. She didn't think he really cared about her or wanted her. "God, along with everyone else, seemed very far away," she said.

This failure to understand God's love distorted her perspective, her personality, her very being. She continued the account of her humiliation on Parents' Night:

Seeing that I was standing alone on the dance floor in front of all the parents and my peers, the dance instructor came over to be my partner. At the end of several dances, she announced to the crowd, "Well, boys, you may not want to date Sophie, but if you want to win next week's dance competition, you should pick her as your partner."

That was a voice I heard over and over again. It confirmed who I would always be. I would never be desirable, but I could be useful. The only reason someone would want to be with me would be if I could help them accomplish something or make them look good.

So I worked hard at being responsible, capable, helpful. In all my busy striving, God seemed both distant and demanding. I concluded that God may be out there, but I would need to take care of myself and do all I could on my own to ensure that I was not standing on the dance floor alone ever again.

Then came that moment at a college retreat. The speaker said at the end of his prayer, "God is here. How is he reaching out to you?"

In that moment of prayer, Sophie saw Jesus. She told me, "He was coming to me and just for me. As Jesus walked toward me, he extended his hand to me. When I reached out with my hand toward his, he invited me to dance. Jesus was right before me, calling my name, asking me with delight to come just as I was into his arms and dance."

Do you want to find God? Sophie would assure you, and Jon and I do too, that he's reaching out to you, loving you despite everything you've done and everything you've been through. He wants to take your hand. He'll enclose you in an embrace of perfect love and acceptance.

13

Your New I.D.

With his wife, Lena, my friend Jared was on a luxury cruise to the Bahamas that he had won for being a top producer in his company. Others in his company were on the cruise as well. They arrived back in Fort Lauderdale early in the morning and docked. Just as it was time to wake up—*Bam, bam, bam!* Someone was beating on their cabin door. Lena was closest to the door and opened it a crack.

The crack was all it took. Six Drug Enforcement Administration agents stormed in, wearing bulletproof vests and pointing semiautomatic weapons at Jared, who was sitting on the bed in his underwear. Can you imagine the shock?

"What, what, what?!" Jared yelled.

"Don't move, sir!" an agent shouted. "You are under arrest." The agents had warrants for his arrest in six states for dealing cocaine.

The hallway outside Jared and Lena's room began to fill up with executives from Jared's company wondering what was going on.

"I had no idea why the DEA cops were there," Jared said later. "It completely bamboozled me. Obviously they had the wrong guy, and I was going to have to straighten this out somehow. But maybe even worse was the fact that I knew instantly what my boss and coworkers were thinking—that I must be some kind of bad guy. My heart just sank."

Jared had been a victim of identity theft. Without his knowledge, someone had acquired his Social Security and credit card numbers. This same someone was engaged in distinctly illegal activities.

It took two hours for Jared to convince the DEA agents that they had the wrong guy and they should let him go. Then it took him weeks of difficult conversations with his company leaders to make sure they understood the whole story. Along the way, he spent thousands of dollars in attorney fees to get his name cleared.

Jared found out how unsettling, and costly, it can be to lose your identity.

In a way, identity theft is what happened to the son in Jesus's story. Here's what I mean: He left home in search of love, purpose, meaning, pleasure—all those things we're looking for when we have the feeling, *There's got to be more.* But to get the "more" he wanted, he had to trade away his family inheritance. No wonder that by the time he came to his senses, he hardly recognized himself and had forgotten where he had come from and all that came with it. His poor choices had robbed him of his true understanding of himself.

I remember an old southern orator saying, "Be who you is, because if you ain't who you is, you is who you ain't." The lost son became who he ain't.

Then came the startling embrace and the unexpected welcome home by the father, followed by the son's reaction. Do you see his stolen-identity problem in his anguished words, "I am no longer worthy to be called your son"? That's a problem many of us face when we come home to the heavenly Father.

This chapter takes a look at your true I.D. from *the other side* of that pivotal event—from the side you're on now if you've received and responded to the Father's love. And something has changed in a big way. You *do* have a new identity.

But how? And who exactly are you now?

Let's start with the awakening you've been praying: *Awaken in me the awareness that I am your unconditionally loved child.* What does it mean to be unconditionally loved by your heavenly Father?

CLOTHED IN ACCEPTANCE

While the son was still shaking his head, insisting, "I am no longer worthy to be called your son," the father shouted to a servant,

> *Quick! Bring the best robe and put it on him. Put a ring on his finger and sandals on his feet.*[77]

You can imagine that the son's head was spinning. "Robe? Ring? Sandals? Uh . . . for me?" Each of these gifts from the father was a proof of his love, and each conveyed a powerful meaning in that culture. I'll take them one at a time.

—*Robe: A symbol of rest.* At the father's command, the servants bring the best robe and put it on the son. What is the best robe in the house? Of course it is the father's robe. The father does not give him an old robe or an extra robe he has in the closet. He gives his son his own robe.

But as this is happening, I picture the son saying, "No, no . . . you don't know where I've been. You don't know what I've done. What you gave me— it's all gone!" But still, the father drapes the best robe around his shoulders.

And as the robe envelops him, the son feels a sense of rest coming over him. He doesn't have to run. He doesn't have to prove himself. He doesn't have to strive. Everything is going to be okay. This is what home feels like.

Now he can rest.

—Ring: A symbol of security. Next, the father places a ring on the son's finger. Throughout history, if you were in the presence of a king, you would kiss his ring because it was symbolic of his power. Presenting a ring to someone was a sign of being placed in an office of authority. Among the rich it was a sign of dignity and wealth. Kings and pharaohs used a signet ring to stamp royal decrees and make them official.

Do you see what is happening here? The giving of the ring transfers from the father to the son all his power and authority. The son who was broke and penniless now had the father's financial identity he could leverage as his own. It would be like a father giving his son or daughter a credit card. As the son looked at the ring, he knew he need never go without a meal again, never go without a place to sleep, never want anything. The ring sealed his identity and brought him tremendous security.

—Sandals: A symbol of acceptance. In an ancient Jewish home, the only people who would wear sandals in the house were the homeowners. Slaves and servants went barefoot.

But shoeless is how I imagine the son returned home. He came home destitute, looking more like a servant or slave than a son. When the father gave sandals to his son, he was symbolically and publicly saying, "Welcome home. You're not a slave. You're my son. We are family."

These three gifts reveal that his true identity had been restored to him. Struggle as he might to accept it, he also knew it was his to enjoy. Who is he *really*? Well, he's *not* a loser or a stranger. He is a son again. He is part of the family. That is his new I.D.!

With the robe, the ring, and the sandals transforming his appearance, the son may have wanted to stammer like my friend Jared did when his identity was in question, "What, what, what?!"

But he didn't get the chance. The father in the story went on to call out,

Bring the fattened calf and kill it. Let's have a feast and celebrate. For this son of mine was dead and is alive again; he was lost and is found.[78]

From dead to alive, from lost to found? That calls for a party! And that's what happens in the story. The father invites friends and family from far and near to celebrate with dancing, singing, and great food.

My guess is that sometime during that epic celebration, while the son was enjoying the food and his new clothes, he had his moment of full awakening to his father's love. *I am my father's deeply, unconditionally loved son!* Looking around, he finally grasped that by grace his past has been redeemed. The story about who he used to be, and what he did, and who he is now is—get this—the reason for the party!

Where's the shame in that?

"THAT KID IS AMAZING!"

Rick Hoyt is confined to a wheelchair and has no control over his muscle functions. At birth Rick was strangled by the umbilical cord, leaving him brain damaged and unable to control his limbs. When Rick was eight months old, the doctors told his parents, "Put him in an institution, he'll be nothing but a vegetable for the rest of his life."[79]

Rick's parents weren't buying it. They noticed the way Rick's eyes followed them around the room.

Then when Rick was eleven, his parents took him to the engineering department at Tufts University and asked if there was anything to help the boy communicate.

They were told that there was nothing going on in Rick's brain.

His father, Dick, asked the engineers to tell Rick a joke.

They did.

Little Rick laughed.

It turns out a lot was going on in his brain. Rigged up with a computer that allowed him to control the cursor by touching a switch with the side of his head, Rick was finally able to communicate. First words? "Go Bruins!"

When Rick learned about a benefit race for a college student who was paralyzed in an accident, he pecked out a request to do the run.

His dad pushed Rick in his wheelchair the entire five miles. After the race Rick typed for his father, "Dad, when I'm running it feels like I'm not handicapped." That sentence was all the motivation Rick's dad needed.

By 2014, Team Hoyt had completed one thousand races, including marathons, duathlons, and triathlons. Six were Ironman competitions.

Rick is also a college graduate, earning a degree in special education from Boston University in 1993.[80]

People who know Rick Hoyt look at him today like he's a superhero. Nobody looks at him and says, "There is that handicapped kid . . . too bad." People look at him for motivation and speak of his accomplishments with admiration.

Everybody knows about Rick Hoyt. Know why? Because he had a father who loved him. Dick Hoyt loved his son so much that it changed his son's identity. Rick felt like his disability disappeared.

FULLY RESTORED

The Bible has many things to say about how your identity has been fully restored if you have come home to God through Jesus. Do you want to know a few of them? You're going to like this.

You are not condemned (bye-bye, shame!).[81]

You can never be separated from God's love.[82]

You are God's child.[83]

You have every spiritual blessing.[84]

Your sins have been forgiven.[85]

You have been seated in the heavenly realms.[86]

You, after having been far away from God, have been brought near to him.[87]

You will rise from the dead.[88]

This is what awakening to God's love looks like. It changes how you think about him, about yourself, about others. It changes who you are. It changes how you feel.

You know now without a doubt that you have a heavenly Father who loves you deeply and unconditionally. He loves you so much that he has made you one with him in Christ. That old lost you? Gone! You realize you can stop saying, "I don't deserve this." You can start saying, "God loves me deeply after all." You can celebrate the rest, security, and acceptance you now enjoy as his fully restored son or daughter.

So now that your sense of yourself has caught up with the reality, what are you to do?

Just this: You're home—*so live like it.* Look around and see what it means to live the rest of your life like a child of God. The party has just begun.

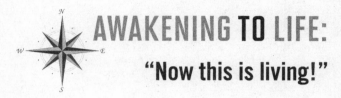

AWAKENING TO LIFE:
"Now this is living!"

This son of mine was dead and is
alive again; he was lost and is found.
—Luke 15:24

14

Partying at the Lost and Found

Before Jesus told the story of the prodigal son, he told two other stories in which someone loses something of great value.

The first story is about a man who has a hundred sheep and loses one of them. He looks and looks for it, and when he finds the sheep, "he calls his friends and neighbors together and says, 'Rejoice with me; I have found my lost sheep.'"[89]

The second story is about a woman who loses a valuable coin. She looks and looks for it, and when she finds it, "she calls her friends and neighbors together and says, 'Rejoice with me; I have found my lost coin.'"[90]

In our day, these losses might be similar to having our retirement savings wiped out in a stock market crash. You can see why the man and the woman were so happy when they got their lost possessions back.

Then comes the third story—our story of the lost son. As we've already seen, when the son finally nears home, his father comes running out to hug and kiss and welcome him home. Then he calls everyone together to make an announcement:

"Let's have a feast and celebrate. For this son of mine was dead and is alive again; he was lost and is found." So they began to celebrate.[91]

I hope you noticed something that happens in all three stories.

When the lost sheep is found, it happens.

When the lost coin is found, it happens.

When the lost son is found, it happens.

What happens? The news goes out—what was lost is now found. It's time to rejoice. And everyone gratefully celebrates!

If you have found your way back to God, then you have good reason to celebrate!

You were lost and now are found.

You have been given the chance to make peace with your past.

You have been given a purpose for living.

You have been given hope for your future.

Celebrate!

LIVING IN THE NEW

You have come to the final awakening on your journey — what Jon and I have labeled the *awakening to life*. Previously, you became aware of your own desires for something more (awakening to longing). Then you began to realize you'd made a mistake in setting your own course in life and wanted to start over (awakening to regret). You also realized that you needed help from God to make a change, and so you came home to him (awakening to help). He welcomed you so fast and so thoroughly that it took you a while to comprehend the grace you'd received (awakening to love). Now you're ready to explore what this life at home with God looks like.

First of all, it's a whole *new* life. The apostle Paul expresses it this way:

Anyone who believes in Christ is a new creation. The old is gone! The new has come![92]

If you're ready to live a new life with the Father, here's the prayer for you:

> God, if you are real,
> make yourself real to me.
> Awaken in me the confidence
> that I can live a brand-new life.

In this chapter and the next two to come, we'll explore your new life as it plays out in three relationships that are vital to all new Christ followers: your relationship with God, your relationship with others, and your relationship with the world. When you're living a new way in these areas, you'll want to declare, "Now *this* is living!"

We start with your relationship with God. Jon and I have found that sons and daughters who have found their way back to God are drawn to both public worship and personal devotions. Previously, these things may have seemed boring or powerless. Now they're not a duty. They're a celebration!

"I Earnestly Search for You"

King David of the Old Testament wrote many psalms, or prayers, where he tried to put words to his relationship with God. Psalm 63 gives us an example of what it can look like for us to live in celebration with God and his people.

O God, you are my God;
  I earnestly search for you.
My soul thirsts for you;
  my whole body longs for you
in this parched and weary land
  where there is no water.
I have seen you in your sanctuary
  and gazed upon your power and glory.
Your unfailing love is better than life itself;
  how I praise you! . . .

I lie awake thinking of you,
  meditating on you through the night.
Because you are my helper,
  I sing for joy in the shadow of your wings.
I cling to you;
  your strong right hand holds me securely.[93]

It's hard to imagine that my relationship with God could ever reach the depth expressed by David. However, if celebrating and relating to God could be like that for you, wouldn't you want it?

Consider this: The moment you utter a prayer of thanksgiving or make a request for help, you have the undivided attention of the Creator of the universe. And when you hold a Bible in your hand, you have at your fingertips the words of God in writing.

MAKING YOUR CELEBRATION PUBLIC

One of the first ideas we discover from this song of David's is that he spent time with God in the company of other sincere spiritual seekers. David says,

I have seen you in your sanctuary.[94]

The sanctuary he's referring to is the temple, where Israelites of his day worshiped together. The comparable type of experience in our day would be a worship service in a church. And another term I sometimes use for a church is "faith family."

Of course, celebrating with any family—God's family included—can be tricky.

When we realized we were going to be adding a third child to our family, Sue and I made plans to tell our six-year-old daughter, Amy, and four-year-old son, Josh. We thought taking them out for ice cream would be a great way to celebrate and break the news. So we ordered ice cream, and I proceeded to tell them, "Guys, we've got some good news!"

They both looked up, eager with anticipation.

Sue continued, "You are going to have a baby brother!"

First there was silence. Then Josh broke the silence. "I wanted a dog!" he said.

Well, I have some good news for you. You may react like my son Josh and be slightly underwhelmed, but the good news is this—as a child of God, you have a family!

You may have thought that this journey back to God is one you take all alone. It's not. You were never designed to travel alone. If you look over your shoulder, you will realize that God has put people on your path to help you find your way back to him. Those people are a part of God's family. And you are now part of this ever-expanding and always-inclusive community of people who love God and are loved in return.

"A PLACE TO CALL HOME"

Holly grew up with a Jewish dad and a Presbyterian mom and didn't feel like she fit in anywhere. She attended both synagogue and church periodically throughout her childhood and teen years, but those experiences left her feeling lost and confused. In college she began dating her future husband, Ben, who attended a Catholic church. Attending church with his family only showed her one more place where she didn't fit in. When they married, they didn't know whether to go to his church or her church, so they mostly didn't go at all.

Then life suddenly got really hard for Holly and Ben. Ben lost his job. They suffered the loss of Ben's mother. They lost most of their life savings to a failed business. They watched their precious new baby endure two surgeries, and Ben was in a terrible car accident that left him partially paralyzed and sinking into a deep depression.

Her husband was at rock bottom, and Holly knew she couldn't let herself join him there. She knew of only one person to turn to, and that was God. She went into her bedroom, got down on her knees, and pleaded with God to show up and help her family out of this horrible mess.

One day soon after she said this prayer, God showed up in a remarkable way: Ben was suddenly motivated. He got off the couch one Sunday morning and told Holly he was going "church shopping." When Ben returned from church that morning, Holly saw that something had changed in him. He wanted to go back, so the next week she and the kids went with him.

Almost immediately Holly knew this was a place where her family could find their way back to God. It was the first time in Holly's life when she felt like she belonged. She recalls, "I remember sitting in that first service and feeling like the message was meant for me. I felt like somebody got me, and that somebody was God. God got me, and he loved me. We still had our struggles, but now I knew we had a place to call home."

So one important and helpful step you can take in your new life with God is to find a faith community with whom you can celebrate. Maybe, like Holly, you tried going to church and never felt like you belonged. Or maybe you found church to be irrelevant and confusing or just plain boring. It could be that you have never been able to get past the fact that too many church-goers you know are one person on Sunday and another on Monday. You may have been a regular churchgoer in the past, but circumstances surfaced that left you feeling that church was no longer a safe place.

My prayer is that you, like Holly and her family, will find a life-giving church where you can celebrate all that God is doing in your life along with other prodigals who are finding their way back to God. When the church is at its best, it is the most life-giving, difference-making community in the world. It's full of people who don't have their act together but willingly acknowledge their need to come together for celebration, learning, and encouragement.

Ask God to help you find a life-giving church where you can celebrate publicly and continue to grow in your relationship with him. It may take some time, but I promise that if you sincerely search for a church home, God will help you find one that is right for you.

Taking Your Celebration Private

A corporate gathering is not the only place for celebration. David also wrote:

> *I lie awake thinking of you,*
> *meditating on you through the night.*[95]

In Psalm 63 he shows us that those times we spend praying on our own include more than asking God for what we want and need. Those times are also meant to be a celebration of God's goodness to us, expressions of our gratitude to him for how he has provided for us or blessed us.

One of the best ways to grow as a follower of Jesus is to make private celebration a daily experience that includes Bible reading, reflection, and prayer. This is true in my experience and observation. It was also recently confirmed by one of the most comprehensive studies ever conducted on spiritual growth, which concluded that the common denominator among people who grow spiritually is "reflection on scripture."[96]

Now, I am easily distracted, so a little routine and a few simple practices help me stay focused.

In my own private times with God, I begin with a brief prayer I learned from Samuel, the Old Testament prophet. He spoke these words to God: "Speak, for your servant is listening."[97] I have realized that if I really want to grow as a Christ follower, I need to hear from God.

The idea of hearing from God may sound like a stretch for you, but the truth is, God still speaks, even today. One of the primary ways he speaks to us is through his Word, the Bible. God also speaks through others who are finding their way back to God, through circumstances, and through his Spirit. Anytime you think you are hearing from God, however, it's crucial that you determine whether what you hear is consistent with what God says in the Bible.

After I pray, "Speak, Lord, your servant is listening," I read a selection of Scripture, using a modern translation of the Bible, such as the New International Version or the New Living Translation. I usually follow a reading guide that gives me a plan for reading a selection from the Bible every day. Other people simply read one chapter of the Bible a day. When people are just getting started, I often recommend starting with the gospel of John, which tells the story of Jesus's life.

As I read a selection of Scripture, I look for one or two verses that I believe God may have in mind specifically for me. It may be a verse that brings me hope in a difficult situation or one that compels me to take action or think about a situation differently than I had before. I try to find at least one verse that I can focus on that day, and then I write it down in a journal or on a notepad. I find it helpful to keep an ongoing record of these verses.

After I finish reading the selection of Scripture and write down the verse that I felt drawn to, I spend a few moments in prayer. My prayer usually includes asking God to help me put into action something from what I read, as well as seeking guidance for my day. I also pray on behalf of any family members and friends who may be in need. I make it a practice to write down these prayers, along with the verse I chose for that day.

It's quite simple, but that's what private celebration looks like for me, and that's how I seek to hear from God every day.

Will you try a similar approach that works for you? I think you'll be surprised by how much encouragement and guidance you will find in the presence of God every day.

GOD DELIGHTS IN YOU

I used to know of an ice cream shop called Dairy Delight. Since I love ice cream, I associate the word *delight* with something I enjoy very much. That may be a reason why one of my favorite verses from the Bible is Psalm 149:4:

The LORD takes delight in his people.

Have you ever considered that God not only loves you and welcomes you home but actually delights in you?

Whether you are celebrating in a quiet place alone or with hundreds of people in a large auditorium, God still feels the same way about you. He delights in you and can't wait to spend time with you. The simple fact that you have welcomed him into your day and chosen to celebrate with him brings him more delight than you could ever imagine.

When we celebrate, we grow in our relationship with God. In the next chapter we'll look at what it means to grow as a follower of Christ in our relationships with others.

15

Better Together

A while back, Edward Hallowell and a team of researchers from the Harvard Medical School discovered that the two most powerful and meaningful experiences in life are achieving (reaching a goal and accomplishing something worthwhile) and connecting (relating to someone in a significant way). According to Hallowell, our society is becoming more and more obsessed with achieving while at the same time becoming increasingly bankrupt when it comes to connecting.[98]

Achieving is not bad, of course, but research shows that it's no substitute for connecting. People who excel at achieving but fail at connecting end up unhappy people. The old saying is true: "Nobody on their deathbed looks back on their life and wishes they'd spent more time at the office."

By contrast, people who prioritize connecting and having meaningful relationships, even if they're not great at achieving and accomplishing goals, still report life as being fulfilling.

In our new life with God, we all need the encouragement and accountability of others in order to grow strong and flourish in this journey. When we intentionally and consistently stay connected to others, we are more likely to experience life as God intended for us to experience it.

An ancient word describes the kind of connection God wants you to experience with others. It's the word *koinonia*. Sometimes in the Bible this ancient word is translated "fellowship."

In *The Fellowship of the Ring,* the first volume of the epic adventure The Lord of the Rings, J. R. R. Tolkien gives us a great picture of what this fellowship is like. You may recall how nine friends band together, deal with their differences, and unite for a life-and-death cause. It is through this adventure that deep bonds of love and friendship are formed. This kind of uniting together of people, when it's empowered by God's Spirit, is the essence of koinonia.

Worship with a church family is crucial. But while such a large gathering is great for celebrating, it's not so good for connecting. That's why I strongly urge everyone to find some kind of small group—a Bible study or other type of group that includes a dozen or so people who are prepared to commit to each other intensely. These groups are small in size but huge in impact.

As Fred Knott found, they can be a lifeline to hold on to in even the worst circumstances.

"They Got Me Through This"

Fred had a hunch he had cancer. How could he know? Ten years before, at the age of twenty-five, he was diagnosed with testicular cancer. As he told me the story, he said, "I just knew. The symptoms were similar to the first time, and the first time it was a lonely, brutal struggle. I was afraid, really afraid." When Fred told his wife, Amanda, she insisted that he go to the hospital immediately. But he wouldn't go.

When she finally did convince him, they went to the hospital and sat in the car. Fred refused to get out. In fact, thirteen times Amanda drove him to the hospital, and thirteen times he would not get out.

It would take more than just Amanda's persuasions to convince Fred to get his condition medically checked out. Thankfully, there were some others in a position to push Fred to do what he needed to do.

About a year before Fred started getting concerned about his cancer returning, his then new bride, Amanda, invited him to go to church with her. Then, just a few weeks prior to his sharing his concern about his health with his wife, his good friend Mike joined a men's group and convinced Fred they should go together.

At one of the group gatherings, Fred was struggling with thoughts that his cancer could be returning. Toward the end of the gathering, Nick, the leader of the group, said, "I want everyone to pray selfishly today. Don't ask us to pray for someone else. Let us know how we can pray for you."

When it was Fred's turn to talk, he surprised himself by what he said out loud. "Guys, I need courage to go see the doctor, but I'm too scared to go." He went on to explain his history of cancer and how he was afraid to go through it again.

The group immediately began to rally around Fred. Several of the guys assured him, "Together we can beat this, but first you've got to call the doctor. If not for yourself, do it for your wife and your family." One guy stepped out of the room and tracked down Fred's oncologist from ten years ago and gave Fred the phone number.

For the first time, Fred followed through and made the appointment. Sadly, the doctors confirmed he had cancer and said he needed to start chemotherapy right away. The day before he started chemo, he pulled that group of men together and was baptized as an expression of his decision to follow Jesus.

This group of fourteen guys continued to rally around Fred.

They gave him courage when he was fearful.

They sponsored a fund-raiser they called Fear Knott Fest, and with more than three hundred people attending, raised thousands of dollars to assist with his medical bills.

They encouraged him emotionally, refusing to let fear stop him.

They challenged him spiritually. When he doubted, they had faith on his behalf.

Fred told me, "Those guys from my Wednesday morning group got me through this."

Eventually Fred and his wife made the decision to move from Illinois to Arizona. This was a tough choice, as they knew it would mean leaving the support of these men. But Amanda was offered a new job there, and doctors insisted the Arizona climate would be better for Fred's health.

In spite of the move, the cancer returned again and again. Fred began to accept the fact that his days were numbered. Through it all, his small group from Chicago continued to stay in touch with him, but Fred also found a new group of guys in Arizona who filled the void left by his friends in Chicago.

When the end seemed near, Nick, the leader from his group in Chicago, flew to Arizona to say his good-byes. Fred wasn't always alert during the visits, but Nick says they had several conversations about death and eternity. Nick told me, "Fred knew he was going to see God." During some of his final moments with Nick, Fred asked him to record a prayer for his children.

When Fred finally passed, there were two services: one in Arizona and one in Chicago. Nick led the memorial service in Chicago. At the end of the service, he played the prayer Fred had recorded for his children. Nick reflected on that moment: "Playing the prayer was a gift from Fred to his children. His journey with God in this life had come to an end. He had fulfilled what he felt God wanted for his life. Playing that prayer confirmed for his children and everyone else that God was very real to Fred."

I love that story and what happens when God draws people together by powerful bonds into a new community. Dallas Willard wrote, "The purpose of God with human history is nothing less than to bring out of it . . . an eternal community of those who were once thought to be just 'ordinary human beings.' . . . God's precreation intention to have that community as a special dwelling place or home will be realized. He will be its prime sustainer and most glorious inhabitant."[99]

Connecting is God's dream for all people. Small groups are an ideal environment in which to incubate that connectedness. If you get the chance to join one (or join one again, if you've dropped out), by all means take it.

SMALL BUT MIGHTY

Recently an online travel company had an ad campaign called Trip a Day Giveaway; the company gave a free trip to one person every day to anywhere in the world. There was only one catch: you had to leave on that very day.

One of the ads showed a guy who did just that. He dropped everything and left for a free trip to the Great Wall of China.[100] I remember looking at that ad and asking myself, *If I were offered a free trip to anywhere in the world, but I had to leave right now, would I go?* I wasn't sure at first. But then I thought, *You know what? I definitely would do it, because it is the opportunity of a lifetime.*

Fred would have told you that being part of a community of people who genuinely love and care for each other was the opportunity of a lifetime. Those relationships are priceless.

I'm not alone in touting the potential of what can happen in a small group of Jesus's followers. Jesus said:

Where two or three gather in my name, there am I with them.[101]

Here Jesus is saying that there's an experience of his presence we can only have in the presence of others. And it doesn't take many.

Jesus himself formed a small group. He gathered twelve men to spend time with him and learn from him. When these disciples finally split up after his death and resurrection, it was like the splitting of an atom—the power burst out over the whole world and is still spreading today as the message of Jesus reaches into every corner of the earth. That's how much power Jesus built into that small group, starting when they were kicking around together back in the first century.

I'm not saying every small group will have the impact of the original group of disciples. But I'll tell you something—over and over again, I have seen people find new hope, purpose, and direction for their lives because of the relationships formed in a small group. For that reason, Jon and I have been in small groups our entire adult lives.

We have seen marriages on the brink of divorce reconciled because of what God did in and through a close-knit community of friends we call a small group.

We have seen people not only survive but thrive during the most difficult of life-and-death circumstances because they were connected to others in a small group.

We have seen thousands of people find their way back to God through small groups.

What about you? Don't you long to connect deeply with others and live out the kind of koinonia God so wants for us?

If your life continues on its current trajectory, will you have given most of your time and energy to connecting with people or only accomplishing goals?

The thought of being in a small group may be intimidating and overwhelming to you. Maybe you can't imagine how you would find the time for one more commitment. It might be that the thought of letting other people in on your personal struggles makes you want to run away as fast as you can. Let me encourage you: I know thousands of people who at one time would never have considered being part of a small group but who now believe it is the opportunity of a lifetime and a vital part of their journey as Christ followers.

If I haven't been unmistakably clear about this, let me be now: You need other people to help you find your way back to God. Until you try it, you'll never know the big impact of a small group.

BLESSED BY A BUNCH OF GUYS

A friend of mine was in a small group that gathered every week. It was made up of couples in their early thirties, with the exception of one couple in their sixties. At the end of their gatherings, the group would break out into two smaller groups for prayer—men in one group, women in another.

One evening, the husband of the couple in their sixties told the men in the group how he really wanted to buy a Christmas gift for his daughter, from whom he'd become estranged, but that his life-insurance premium was also due and he couldn't afford to cover both costs. He asked the guys to pray for him about this difficult choice he had to make. He was in a quandary because he wanted to reconcile with his daughter and was seriously considering sacrificing his life insurance in order to do it.

After the group gathered that night, the guys got together and decided to pitch in to cover the cost of this man's life-insurance premium. It wasn't a lot of money for them, but to this older gentleman, it was a significant part of his income.

The following week, the younger men gave him enough money so he wouldn't have to sacrifice his life insurance. When they handed him the cash, he looked at the floor, began to shake, and started to cry. He said he'd never received anything like this before and felt so blessed that a bunch of guys half his age were willing to share with him in such a profound way.

When the men in this group agreed to pay for his life-insurance premium, they had no idea that two months later he would die of a massive heart attack. Because of their generous act, he was reconciled to his daughter and he was able to provide financially for his wife after he died. The man's wife asked the group to plan and lead her husband's memorial service.

What a beautiful picture of connecting! Even in the shadow of death, this is living!

TAKING A CHANCE ON COMMUNITY

Somebody once told me, "I hear all this talk about how much God loves me, but I still don't *feel* like he loves me." Maybe you feel that way. You've been told that he loves you, and you want to believe he loves you, but you just don't feel like it. The reason so many of us never feel the love of God is because God wants us to know and experience his love through the love of other people. Sadly, too often we don't let ourselves get close enough to other people to feel his love through them.

Here's my challenge to you: As you're praying for God to awaken new life in you, dare to take a step forward and connect with a small group of people who, like you, are finding their way back to God. When you open yourself up to that kind of community, God's love will flow through you and to you in ways you never knew possible. As a result, you will begin to contribute to the lives of people around you like never before.

16

Your Part in God's Dream

God has a dream for this world, and you're invited to be a part of it. It is an irresistible dream that God has had for all eternity. It's a dream for your life, your community, and the whole world.

God's dream is that you would live each second of your existence with a confidence that he relentlessly and passionately loves you. His dream is that you would willingly risk loving others because you know God has risked everything in loving you.

I've often wondered how the son who returned to his father lived from that day forward. Jesus's story ends before we find out. I don't think he looked on a hungry man or woman in the same way again. Or listened to someone's story of failure and loss with judgment. Or thought his father's wealth was all about buying him more status or comfort. Do you?

When we truly awaken to the new life God offers at home with him, we see the possibilities for our future completely differently. We exclaim, "Now *this* is living!" but we realize that "living" means something different now. It means living a life that is better, bigger, and more meaningful than ever before.

DEEPLY COMMITTED TO HELPING OTHERS

We've looked at celebrating (relationship with God) and connecting (relationship with others) in the preceding chapters. The third relationship that is vital to living with God is all about contributing. Contributing is primarily about growing in our relationship with the world. It means, for one thing, that we feel deeply committed to helping others find their way back to God and to restoring our world to the dream God had for it from the beginning.

In probably the most famous line from the Bible, Jesus said,

God so loved the world that he gave his one and only Son,
that whoever believes in him shall not perish but have eternal
life.[102]

This line is rightly famous because it is so profound. It is out of a love for our world—the physical world and the people who live in this world—that God made the ultimate contribution, giving up the life of his very own Son.

Likewise, God wants us to so love the world, and be so grateful to him for what he has done for us, that we can't wait to give back. He says, "I want you to fully contribute by discovering how your passions intersect with the deep needs of the world that I love so much."

Wouldn't you like to be about a mission so compelling that you can't wait to contribute your time, talent, and resources to see it accomplished?

Can you imagine what it would be like to work alongside others who have found their way back to God, being in the trenches together, making a real difference in the world?

GOAL: RESCUE THREE MILLION CHILDREN

As a kid, Jeff tagged along with his mom to various churches and old-school tent revival meetings. He never really knew God, but he did find enough religious rules to keep him well behaved and out of trouble—that is, until he left home at age seventeen and started hanging around with a rough crowd.

One night, in his search for a new high, he decided to try heroin, but he and his friends couldn't find any. He recalls, "We were driving around in the middle of the night searching for a heroin dealer, and I saw a tent that said, 'Christ Is The Answer.' I shook my head. I'd been there, done that. Besides, I needed more than answers. I needed a purpose and a passion."

Jeff and his friends never found heroin, but he was so trashed by the end of the night that he had to crawl up his driveway to make it into his house. He collapsed in his room and cried out, "God, I don't know where you are, or who you are, or if you're even real, but change my life. It's now or never!" Then he passed out.

He says that he woke up seven hours later, and everything felt strangely different. His mom invited him to the "Christ Is The Answer" tent meeting he had seen the night before. At the meeting, Jeff heard the preacher teaching from these words of Jesus: "If you try to hang on to your life, you will lose it. But if you give up your life for my sake, you will save it."[103] The preacher then gave an altar call, asking people to come forward if they wanted to follow Jesus.

In that moment, Jeff felt like God spoke his own words back to him from his prayer the night before: "It's now or never, Jeff!" He knew it had to be now. So he went forward and prayed, and for the first time he knew he had found his way back to God in Jesus.

Two days later Jeff sold everything he owned. Seven days later, he went to Saint Louis to work with people on the streets. Two weeks after that, he met a missionary in Saint Louis who wanted to bring him to the Philippines. Jeff went, and he's been in the Philippines for more than thirty years.

Jeff started a nonprofit ministry in the Philippines that includes a school, a prison ministry, a hospital visitation program, a mission that rescues children off the streets, a network of new churches, and several economic development initiatives. Jeff's greatest passion is to rescue the millions of children living on the streets of the Philippines, many with nothing to eat and only the clothes on their backs.

A while back, Jeff and Jon were talking, and Jon asked him, "You are over thirty years into this, Jeff. So what's your dream now?"

He replied, "I'd like to get every homeless kid off the streets of the Philippines."

Jon asked, "How many kids are on the streets?"

Jeff said, "About three million."

And then Jon asked him, "How do you respond when people say that's impossible?"

He shrugged, smiled, and said, "Maybe it is, but nobody has ever tried."

How about you? What can you do to participate in God's work of loving the world?

I know the desire is in you. The passion is in you. The motivation is there. The challenge is making the mission so tangible that you can put it into practice every single day.

Let me bring up a word that describes how to love the people and places we come across every single day:

Bless.

The Secret Power of Blessers

Long before Jesus told the story of the prodigal son, God told the biblical patriarch Abraham this:

> *I will bless you;*
> *I will make your name great,*
> *and you will be a blessing. . . .*
> *All peoples on earth*
> *will be blessed through you.*[104]

God blessed Abraham relationally, financially, and spiritually. The point of that blessing was not for him to merely receive the blessings. God blessed Abraham—and all who follow after him as God's children—to bless others. If you have found your way back to God and are his child, then you are being blessed to be a blessing. When we contribute our time, talent, and resources, we bless the people and places around us.

In his book *The Missional Entrepreneur,* Mark Russell refers to a study of two teams of long-term missionaries who went to Thailand.[105] He called one team the "converters" because they went with the sole intention of evangelizing everyone around them. He called the other team "blessers" because they went just with the intention of doing good for people. The blessers would say, "I'm just here to serve whoever comes my way" or "I just want to be a blessing to the people in the community."

The study followed both teams for a couple of years, and here are two interesting observations: First of all, the blessers had a greater social impact than the converters. Second—and here is what was so surprising—they discovered that the blessers also had almost fifty times as many conversions as the converters!

Maybe this should not be so surprising to us after all. Abraham's example shows us the way. Being a blessing has always been God's strategy for changing the world. And more often than not, the place you and I should begin to change the world is right here, staring us in the face.

CHALK THE BLOCK

One morning Rich was sitting by a café window praying that God would let him bring hope to his Edgewater neighborhood in Chicago. He watched people pass by on their way to work, and he thought they looked like "the zombie parade," as he put it. Everyone was looking down at the sidewalk. People appeared to move forward through their day without life or purpose.

As he prayed, an idea came to him: *What if I could put messages of hope on the sidewalk? Everyone would see them! I could use sidewalk chalk!* Rich named his idea Chalk the Block.

He and a few friends started going out at night and writing messages in sidewalk chalk, especially near commuter stations, bus stops, and major intersections. They added a hashtag and wrote creative messages such as these:

"You could live a good story."

"Would your ten-year-old self like who you have become?"

"Your yesterday does not define your today."

"Maybe what you are holding on to is holding you back."

"All things can be made new."

"You were meant for amazing things."

Like any idea that comes from God, it was powerful. The feedback they received was astounding. People were being inspired and encouraged by these simple messages. People started taking pictures of the sidewalk chalk. Other people wanted to join this little movement. A DePaul University student produced a video documentary.[106] The *Chicago Tribune* published a story.[107] It was amazing! And people were finding their way back to God.

People like Keisha.

"HERE IS THE WORLD"

It was a cold March day in Chicago, one of those days when the snow has cleared but the wind chill makes it feel twenty degrees colder. Keisha left for work feeling melancholy. As she walked to the commuter train station, she began to draw further into herself. With her head down, she crossed the street and noticed brightly colored words that Rich and his friends chalked the night before. On the sidewalk someone had written, "Here is the world, beautiful and terrible things will happen. Do not be afraid."

Keisha had moved back to the Windy City a few months earlier and was trying to reacclimate to living there. Everything was stressing her out: finances, her job, and the e-mail she had received at work the day before from her abusive ex. She knew that message on the sidewalk was for her. She walked on toward the commuter station with tears stinging her eyes and a lump in her throat, but she held her head up and kept her gaze ahead.

Over the next few days, she thought about that message on the sidewalk: "Do not be afraid." She wondered who had written it and how it was there exactly when she needed it. They were powerful words—words she could draw strength from. Words she needed. She wrote them in her journal and would say them to herself when she started to feel overwhelmed or sad about the path her life had taken. The words on the sidewalk gave her hope.

She decided to investigate who wrote the words on the sidewalk. She searched online and quickly came across a church community. She was surprised that a church group was chalking messages on the sidewalk. She decided to check them out in person. She had not been to church since she was a teenager, and deciding to go again was a huge step for her. But when she went for a service, she could feel the love of God so openly that she wanted to be there and get involved.

Since then, she has become a part of this community. "Now I know where this hope is all coming from," she says. "God working through my church, and through my new friends."

All this came from the simple yet creative idea Rich had for bringing a jolt of hope to the lives of emotional zombies.

A Ministry for All Christ Followers

God wants us to be engaged with others. He wants us to never lose our wonder at the gift of his undeserved welcome and desire for others to experience it. Earlier we saw what 2 Corinthians 5:17 says about awakening to life. Here it is again with verses 18–20, asking us to help others find their way back.

> *Anyone who believes in Christ is a new creation. The old is gone! The new has come! It is all from God. He brought us back to himself through Christ's death on the cross. And he has given us the task of bringing others back to him through Christ.*
>
> *God was bringing the world back to himself through Christ. He did not hold people's sins against them. God has trusted us with the message that people may be brought back to him.*[108]

Another way of putting this is to say that when we have found our way back to God, we should do what we can to help others find their way back too. No one wants to be harangued by a "converter." But if we're a "blesser" to others, they'll be better off—and there's a good chance they will find their way home.

If you don't want to take my word about your potential to be a blessing, that's okay. You might, though, believe someone who's been poised on the brink of eternity for years.

DEATHBED MESSENGER

Eight years ago I sat in Lane's living room where hospice workers had placed a bed to make him comfortable for his last days on this earth. He asked me to come over because it was time to plan his funeral. As he told me what he wanted to have said, sung, and celebrated at his memorial, I couldn't help but think back to just a few years earlier when Lane found his way back to God.

Lane was a type-A, driven personality who would start his workday at 5 a.m. and not finish till late in the evening. His obsessive hard work paid off as his company went from being a $100-million business when he started to being worth more than $9 billion when he stepped down because of a terminal illness. The illness brought this ambitious workaholic to a complete stop. When Lane paused long enough to reflect on his life and success, he realized there was something very important missing.

As a kid, his parents took him to church and he had a genuine faith in God, but Lane realized that in his unbridled pursuit of success, God had gradually become a faint and forgotten memory. That was when we met.

Lane was sick. The kind of sick that would slowly kill him. But until it did kill him, it would torture his body with constant pain sixteen hours a day. The illness was his wake-up call that something was missing and he needed God. Lane told me, "Dave, the best thing that ever happened to me was getting sick. From the time I got sick, it refocused me. It caused me to find my way back to God and feel so close to God. I would give up everything for what I have now."

I still have the notes for Lane's funeral. They have gone unused. It has been nearly a decade since hospice was called, and Lane hasn't died yet. But neither has Lane been cured. He is in pain every day of his life and only has energy to go out for a meal and spend a little time online exchanging e-mails. Since his spiritual rebirth, Lane has also found a new identity. He's not a workaholic creating his own kingdom. Instead, he is a messenger sharing his story and helping others find their way back to God.

The experience of being brought back from dead to alive, from lost to found will do that to you!

Since planning his funeral, Lane more than anyone has encouraged me to write this book. He is still alive and living one day at a time as God's messenger. I asked him what he would say to you and me. Here it is in his words:

> I know that life is but a minute in God's eternity. So we must take the time we have and make the most of it. Each of us has friends that are aching for peace. Each of us knows people who are dealing with health conditions, loss of jobs, divorces, problems with kids—you name it and someone has it.
>
> Do not be nervous in your efforts. Pray to God that he will use you as his messenger. Ask God to give you the words to write or say. I know everyone doesn't have the time I do now, but all of us can take time every day to reach out to one person.
>
> It is my plan to do this until the day I die. If I can help anyone to take that first step back to God, I will. My life seemed good for years, but I was missing that personal relationship with God. Now I have found it and it is so important. My hope is for everyone I care about, everyone I know, to find their way back to God too.

Lane has the same mission in life that I do: hpftwbtG. I'll tell you, there's nothing that will confirm your new life more than helping others find new life too. There's nothing like helping others find their way back to God.

Finding Your Way Back to God...
Again and Again

You have prayed the prayer, "God, if you are real, make yourself real to me." You have been seeking God. And if you haven't already found God, Jon and I believe you will find him soon.

Wager won!

But before we finish, I want to remind you of something.

Although God promises "Never will I leave you,"[109] there may be times along the way when God will seem distant. The detachment may be the result of neglecting your relationship with God for a season. It might be that you go through tremendous hardship and he doesn't seem to answer your prayer.

When you feel the distance growing between you and God, we encourage you to reflect on the five awakenings we described. Whatever your circumstance or difficulty at the time, wherever you have strayed, they will show you the way back to him.

Awakening to Longing: **"There's got to be more."**
We all have a longing to love and be loved in return, to find purpose for our

days, and to make sense out of life when life doesn't make sense. That longing is from God, and when you allow that strong desire for more to draw you nearer to him, he will fulfill your longings.

God knows your needs and desires even better than you do, and he has a life of meaning and passion in mind for you. The "more" you need most can only be found as you continually bring your life back to your heavenly Father.

Let your longings for more—no matter how intense—draw you closer to him instead of pushing you away.

Awakening to Regret: "I wish I could start over."

When we seek to fulfill our longing for love, purpose, and meaning on our own, we repeatedly find disappointment. The regret we feel for taking our own route can either lead to more longing and regret (a cycle from which many people never escape) or motivate us to seek help from the One who can help us most.

You don't have to waste the power of your sincere regret on more self-condemnation and stuckness. You can let it move you confidently in God's direction.

Because now you know the truth, and it's a truth that you can put to work in your life over and over again in the years ahead: With God, we can *always* start over.

Awakening to Help: "I can't do this on my own."

Until we admit that we are powerless on our own to find fulfillment in this life, we will never truly find our way back to God. But once we recognize our need for help, we have already made the turn that leads us home to our heavenly Father.

If you're like every other person we know, you'll try to go it on your own many times in the years to come. Perhaps many times each day, if you're like Jon and me. You'll even try to please and serve God on your own—and that won't work either.

But you and I *can't* do it on our own—and that's a very good thing to know.

Let your awakening to your need for help continue to shape your choices in the years ahead. Now you know that help has a name. His name is Jesus. And he will never leave you. Every time you turn away from self-centeredness and pride, he will be there to rescue, strengthen, and guide you on your journey with him.

Awakening to Love: "God loves me deeply after all."

We experience the irresistible love of God in Jesus when we finally return home to our Father. You have returned, so now you know what we're talking about. There's just nothing that matters more in our lives with God than his everlasting, unconditional love for us. The forgiveness and grace that he offers to every one of us is something we can't find anywhere else. It's almost shocking. It's overwhelming. It is continually amazing. And it is what we truly long for and were made to experience.

As we really awaken to God's love in our lives, some of the choices that seemed impossible before gradually become possible. Trusting God through the ups and downs of life becomes possible. Becoming more like his Son, Jesus Christ, becomes possible—and our deepest desire.

And there's more: Believing in his faithful care for us and those we love makes absolute sense, and infuses our days with God's peace. And knowing that not only does he love us but he loves everyone in the world just as deeply compels us to share the good news with others.

That's the wonder of God's deep love for you and me. It has the power to heal us, change us, energize our hopes and dreams, and motivate us to serve him with our whole lives.

Our advice? From this day forward, live boldly in his love. Never let doubt and discouragement take away what you know to be true!

Awakening to Life: "Now this is living!"

Your new, lifelong walk with Jesus is a journey you never need travel alone. In fact, you never need to live apart from your heavenly Father again. If you find yourself drifting into complacency, looking for substitutes, thinking you have all the answers you need for yourself . . . you know what to do.

Come back to the life that is really living! You know the way, and home is where you always belong.

Be prepared in the years ahead for a kind of life that's different from anything you thought possible when you made a U-turn on the road that day and asked the Father for help. Jon and I have found it to be true, and so have millions of others: the awakening to life brings with it unexpected influence and opportunities. How can this be? It's because Christ is alive in you, and that changes just about everything. Now you can bring hope where there has been discouragement. Now you can show prisoners the way to freedom. Now you can be light in the darkness.

And *that* is living!

So we encourage you to find your place in the community of other grateful sons and daughters of the Father. Connect with them, learn from them, and work alongside them to make a difference for good in marriages, homes, schools, workplaces, and communities.

And together, let's keep helping others find their way back to God. That's where the real celebration is waiting.

God wants to be found by you more than you want to find him. That's why we can promise that, if you seek him with an open heart and an open mind, you will find him. He'll make himself known to you.

There's no universal timetable for crossing the distance to God. Sometimes it happens quickly, and sometimes it happens over months and years. But we have found that, for many people, taking a methodical, daily approach over a relatively short—but not too short—period of time is just right.

So consider using this thirty-day guide. All you need to do is set aside fifteen minutes or so per day to reflect on a personal question, record some of your thoughts, and pray one of the five simple prayers taught in *Finding Your Way Back to God*. We believe that the process will take you all the way from feeling miserable about being distant from God to feeling full of joy, *knowing* you are his unconditionally loved child!

If you want to believe this claim is true but you're not so sure it is, our advice is that you take a bet that it *is* true. Make a wager with God by praying this prayer:

> God, if you are real,
> make yourself real to me.

What have you lost if we're wrong and God doesn't make himself real to you? A few minutes of your time. But if you win the wager, the payoff will be the most important relationship you could ever have.

AWAKENING TO LONGING

As the deer pants for streams of water,
    so my soul pants for you, my God.
My soul thirsts for God, for the living God.
    When can I go and meet with God?
My tears have been my food
day and night,
    while people say to me all day long,
    "Where is your God?"
These things I remember
    as I pour out my soul:
how I used to go to the house of God
    under the protection of the Mighty One
with shouts of joy and praise
    among the festive throng.

Why, my soul, are you downcast?
    Why so disturbed within me?
Put your hope in God,
    for I will yet praise him,
    my Savior and my God.

                —Psalm 42:1–5

Day 1

Think.

How did you forget about God?

Journal.

In a notebook or on your computer, write a brief history of how you grew distant from God (if in fact you ever felt close to him in the first place). Describe how you feel about God right now and why you want to find him.

Pray.

"God, if you are real, make yourself real to me. Awaken in me the ability to see that you are what's missing from my life."

Day 2

Think.

How has your life disappointed you, leaving you saying, "There's got to be more"?

Journal.

Record a few of the bigger disappointments in your life. Also, describe your longing for something more or something better to come in the years that still lie ahead for you.

Pray.

"God, if you are real, make yourself real to me. Awaken in me the ability to see that you are what's missing from my life."

Day 3

Think.

What have been the high points and the low points in your quest to find love?

Journal.

Write down your answer to today's "Think" question, then describe why you keep on looking for love. Be sure to include your longing for God's love.

Pray.

"God, if you are real, make yourself real to me. Awaken in me the ability to see that you are what's missing from my life."

Think.

Would you say that your life has a fulfilling purpose?

Journal.

If you would answer yes to the question above, identify your life's purpose. If you would answer no, describe the desire you feel for greater meaning and purpose. How does this desire motivate your search for God?

Pray.

"God, if you are real, make yourself real to me. Awaken in me the ability to see that you are what's missing from my life."

Day 5

Think.

What are some of the hard things in life that have made you cry out in anguish, "Why, God? Why would you allow this to happen?"

Journal.

If hardships and injustices have contributed to your sense of distance from God, describe how that has come about. If they have fueled your desire for God, describe that too.

Pray.

"God, if you are real, make yourself real to me. Awaken in me the ability to see that you are what's missing from my life."

Day 6

Think.

How does the world's inability to satisfy your deepest longings make you want God more?

Journal.

Describe how dissatisfaction and desire have moved you along in your search to find God.

Pray.

"God, if you are real, make yourself real to me. Awaken in me the ability to see that you are what's missing from my life."

AWAKENING TO REGRET

This is what the LORD says—
  he who made a way through the sea,
  a path through the mighty waters,
who drew out the chariots and horses,
  the army and reinforcements together,
and they lay there, never to rise again,
  extinguished, snuffed out like a wick:
"Forget the former things;
  do not dwell on the past.
See, I am doing a new thing!
  Now it springs up; do you not perceive it?
I am making a way in the wilderness
  and streams in the wasteland.
The wild animals honor me,
  the jackals and the owls,
because I provide water in the wilderness
  and streams in the wasteland,
to give drink to my people, my chosen,
  the people I formed for myself
  that they may proclaim my praise.

— Isaiah 43:16–21

Day 7

Think.

What things make you say, "I wish I could start over"?

Journal.

Describe your biggest regrets and the areas of your life today where you know things could and ought to be better.

Pray.

"God, if you are real, make yourself real to me. Awaken in me the possibility that with you I could start over again."

Day 8

Think.

Would you say you are living more of a *bios* life (just getting by day to day) or a *zoe* life (an eternal quality of life in the here and now)?

Journal.

What is it about the quality of your life that you wish were different? Describe what it is about *zoe* (described in chapter 7) that you wish you had.

Pray.

"God, if you are real, make yourself real to me. Awaken in me the possibility that with you I could start over again."

Day 9

Think.

Do you think often about what will happen to you after death? What role does this wondering play in your desire to find God?

Journal.

Describe your beliefs about what happens after death and how people gain entrance to heaven. Identify any fears or doubts or questions you have about the eternal state that awaits you.

Pray.

"God, if you are real, make yourself real to me. Awaken in me the possibility that with you I could start over again."

Day 10

Think.

Would you say that you are stuck in the place between wanting to start over and actually doing something about it?

Journal.

Identify the things that may be keeping you stuck at a point of merely wanting to start over. Is it not knowing what to do? Being too busy and distracted? Being too discouraged? Not having enough faith? Something else?

Pray.

"God, if you are real, make yourself real to me. Awaken in me the possibility that with you I could start over again."

Day 11

Think.

What do you think the turnaround of repentance would mean for you (see chapter 8)?

Journal.

If you want a new start in life, what do you need to turn from? To whom would you turn? How would you go about making the radical turnaround of repentance? Write about these things.

Pray.

"God, if you are real, make yourself real to me. Awaken in me the possibility that with you I could start over again."

Day 12

Think.

Are you ready to start over?

Journal.

Describe how you feel about turning to God and seeing a real change in your circumstances at last.

Pray.

"God, if you are real, make yourself real to me. Awaken in me the possibility that with you I could start over again."

AWAKENING TO HELP

God so loved the world that he gave his one and only Son, that whoever believes in him shall not perish but have eternal life. For God did not send his Son into the world to condemn the world, but to save the world through him. Whoever believes in him is not condemned, but whoever does not believe stands condemned already because they have not believed in the name of God's one and only Son. This is the verdict: Light has come into the world, but people loved darkness instead of light because their deeds were evil. Everyone who does evil hates the light, and will not come into the light for fear that their deeds will be exposed. But whoever lives by the truth comes into the light, so that it may be seen plainly that what they have done has been done in the sight of God.

—John 3:16–21

Day 13

Think.

What convinces you that you can't start over in life in your own power alone?

Journal.

Describe the failures you've had in trying to start over in the past, or simply the inabilities you sense in yourself to fulfill the deepest longings of your heart. How are you crying out for help?

Pray.

"God, if you are real, make yourself real to me. Awaken in me the willingness to turn toward you for help."

Think.

One meaning of *repentance* is "to go back where you belong" (see chapter 9). Where do you belong?

Journal.

When you think about God, what does his role as Father mean to you? When you think about God's presence, what does the term *home* say to you? Describe in writing your desire to go home to your heavenly Father.

Pray.

"God, if you are real, make yourself real to me. Awaken in me the willingness to turn toward you for help."

Day 15

Think.

Knowing all that you have done wrong in the past, how do you think God will receive you if you come home to him?

Journal.

Do you perceive God to be an angry judge, waiting to exact retribution for your sins? Is he a distant being who doesn't really care about you? Is he an old softy who will let you off the hook with no consequences of any sort, regardless of what you've done? Or is he something else to you? How does your perception of him affect your readiness to take the step of repentance?

Pray.

"God, if you are real, make yourself real to me. Awaken in me the willingness to turn toward you for help."

Day 16

Think.

Which statement best describes your reaction to God's grace?

- "I don't believe it."
- "I expect it!"
- "I don't expect it, but I believe it!"

Journal.

Identify your answer to the question above. (Refer to chapter 10 if you need a review of the options.) Give the reason why you answered that way.

Pray.

"God, if you are real, make yourself real to me. Awaken in me the willingness to turn toward you for help."

Day 17

Think.

When you hear that, in Jesus, God is with you and for you and even pursuing you, as chapter 11 says, how do you react?

Journal.

Write a "pen portrait" of who you think Jesus is and what he means to you. Begin by writing, "To me, Jesus is _____."

Pray.

"God, if you are real, make yourself real to me. Awaken in me the willingness to turn toward you for help."

Day 18

Think.

Are you ready to follow Jesus as your way to come home to the heavenly Father?

Journal.

If you are ready to follow Jesus (or recommit to following him, if you've done it before), write out a prayer asking him to be your Leader and to show you the way home to God.

Pray.

"God, if you are real, make yourself real to me. Awaken in me the willingness to turn toward you for help."

AWAKENING TO LOVE

*I kneel before the Father, from whom every family in heaven and on
earth derives its name. I pray that out of his glorious riches he may
strengthen you with power through his Spirit in your inner being, so
that Christ may dwell in your hearts through faith. And I pray that
you, being rooted and established in love, may have power, together
with all the Lord's holy people, to grasp how wide and long and high
and deep is the love of Christ, and to know this love that surpasses
knowledge—that you may be filled to the measure of all the fullness
of God.*

—Ephesians 3:14–19

Day 19

Think.

When you think about God's welcome of you as his child, do you sometimes have the reaction "I don't deserve this" because his grace seems incredible?

Journal.

Write about a time (or times) when you have felt that God's grace toward you was too great to comprehend or accept. Explore in your journaling what might be the causes of this resistance to grace.

Pray.

"God, if you are real, make yourself real to me. Awaken in me the awareness that I am your unconditionally loved child."

Day 20

Think.

How does shame linger in your spirit, even after you know you have been forgiven by God?

Journal.

Write down the messages shame whispers to you. Describe how these messages affect you.

Pray.

"God, if you are real, make yourself real to me. Awaken in me the awareness that I am your unconditionally loved child."

Think.

What would help you realize that God has wiped your shame and guilt away, totally and permanently?

Journal.

Go back to the shame messages you wrote down yesterday. Now write what you think God might say to contradict these messages.

Pray.

"God, if you are real, make yourself real to me. Awaken in me the awareness that I am your unconditionally loved child."

Day 22

Think.

How does the way you view yourself compare with the way God views you?

Journal.

Writing from God's perspective (just as you did yesterday), complete the phrase "[Your Name Here], to me you are _____."
(For example, "Angela, to me you are a dearly loved child" or "Diego, to me you are holy and pure by my Spirit.") Complete the phrase as many ways as you like, drawing on what you know of God's nature from the Bible.

Pray.

"God, if you are real, make yourself real to me. Awaken in me the awareness that I am your unconditionally loved child."

Day 23

Think.

What indications has God given you that you are now his child?

Journal.

Do you feel that God has spoken to you about his love for you? Has he given you freedom in areas where you once felt bound? Do you have a new peace that you can't explain without God? Record any proof of your new identity in Jesus you have received. Return to this list later when you need encouragement.

Pray.

"God, if you are real, make yourself real to me. Awaken in me the awareness that I am your unconditionally loved child."

Day 24

Think.

Are you at the point of being able to say with conviction, "God loves me deeply after all"?

Journal.

Write about where you are in accepting God's grace—not taking it for granted, but not denying it either. Explore in writing how receiving the overwhelming gift of being God's child has given you spiritual freedom.

Pray.

"God, if you are real, make yourself real to me. Awaken in me the awareness that I am your unconditionally loved child."

AWAKENING TO LIFE

Since . . . you have been raised with Christ, set your hearts on things above, where Christ is, seated at the right hand of God. Set your minds on things above, not on earthly things. For you died, and your life is now hidden with Christ in God. When Christ, who is your life, appears, then you also will appear with him in glory.

— Colossians 3:1–4

Day 25

Think.

How is your life new and different now, compared to when you were feeling so distant from God?

Journal.

Write about the changes God has brought into your new life with him. Also write about the additional changes you hope or expect to see in your new life with the Father.

Pray.

"God, if you are real, make yourself real to me. Awaken in me the confidence that I can live a brand-new life."

Day 26

Think.

What has been your experience with church and church people?

Journal.

If you already have a local church that you're committed to, what can you do to more fully participate in its activities and worship? Or if you are ready to find a church, list the characteristics you'd ideally like it to have (realizing that no church is perfect) and how you can go about finding a church that resembles this portrait.

Pray.

"God if you are real, make yourself real to me. Awaken in me the confidence that I can live a brand-new life."

Day 27

Think.

How do you feel about having a daily time of prayer and Bible reading?

Journal.

Journal about the obstacles that keep you from meeting with the Lord regularly in a time of personal devotions. If you were to get started (or restarted) with a time of Bible reading, reflection, and prayer, what time of day would be best for that? What place would be best? What Bible reading plan would you follow?

Pray.

"God, if you are real, make yourself real to me. Awaken in me the confidence that I can live a brand-new life."

Day 28

Think.

Have you ever been part of a small group of Jesus followers? If so, what was the experience like?

Journal.

How could you find a group of other Jesus followers with whom you could spend time, really get to know, and talk with honestly about your spiritual journey? How might it help in your ongoing desire to live at "home" with your Father? Write down a plan to participate in a small group.

Pray.

"God, if you are real, make yourself real to me. Awaken in me the confidence that I can live a brand-new life."

Day 29

Think.

How do you think God has gifted and called you to serve others?

Journal.

Record some steps you could take to get involved in a form of serving where your joy intersects with the world's needs.

Pray.

"God, if you are real, make yourself real to me. Awaken in me the confidence that I can live a brand-new life."

Day 30

Think.

How many times would you say you have come back to God already in your life?

Journal.

What can you foresee that might make it hard for you to continue living in a sense of closeness with God? What can you do to avoid straying from God (or at least straying so far from God) in the future?

Pray.

"God, if you are real, make yourself real to me. Awaken in me the confidence that I can live a brand-new life."

ACKNOWLEDGMENTS

(Dave) **Sue,** thanks for everything from proofing this book to being my partner and friend from day #1 on this mission. I love you! **Amy,** thanks for your honest and humorous contribution to these pages; your candid approach to spirituality is desperately needed. **Josh,** thank you for your rugged determination; it consistently inspires me to never give up! **Caleb,** thanks for how you love and include people—you have a gift for helping people find their way back to God.

(Jon) **Lisa,** your steadfast encouragement and unwavering love and support are an expression of God's grace to me every day. I love being on this mission with you! **Graham,** your courage and strong character is already helping people find their way back to God. **Chloe,** your heartfelt convictions and ability to skillfully communicate inspire me to keep writing.

Pat Masek, you love this mission every bit as much as we do! Please know that every person who finds his or her way back to God as a result of this book has been directly impacted by your tireless effort.

Amber Stefanski, you live out the mission and message of this book every day. Your selflessness and ability to gracefully juggle so many tasks made writing this book possible.

Thank you, **Mark Sweeney,** for being a good friend as well as a wise sage and trusted guide in the publishing world.

Thank you, **David Kopp.** It quickly became obvious that this book was not only a mission you understood, but also a journey you are living. You are amazing at what you do.

Thank you, **Eric Stanford,** for all of your behind-the-scenes efforts to make *Finding Your Way Back to God* the best that it can be!

Thank you, **Tim Sutherland,** for teaching us that it's not just about "winning souls" but a relationship with God. Your influence is felt in every page of this book.

Thanks, **Eric Bramlett,** for being a brilliant creative force behind this whole project!

Thanks to **Carter Moss** for helping us craft the very best version of each person's "finding their way back to God story."

Thank you **Tammy Melchien, Brian Moll,** and the **teaching team at COMMUNITY** for equipping us and our whole church to help people find their way back to God.

Thanks to the **staff at COMMUNITY;** you have created a place where we see people find their way back to God literally every day (Acts 2:47)!

Thank you to all the **NewThing churches** around the world who were started with this mission: hpftwbtG

Thank you to the team at **Multnomah;** it is great to partner with people who aren't just doing a job but are contributing to the mission.

1. Frank Newport, "More than 9 in 10 Americans Continue to Believe in God," Gallup, June 3, 2011, www.gallup.com/poll/147887/americans-continue-believe-god.aspx.

2. Dan Millman, *Sacred Journey of the Peaceful Warrior* (Tiburon, CA: HJ Kramer, 2004), 53.

3. Jeremiah 29:13.

4. "Father Pleads for Kidnapped Utah Girl," CNN, June 6, 2002, http://edition.cnn.com/2002/US/06/05/utah.teenager/index.html?related.

5. Oliver Libaw, "How Did Abductors Control Elizabeth Smart?" *ABC News*, March 13, 2003, http://abcnews.go.com/US/story?id=90754&page=1.

6. Isaiah 53:6.

7. Joe Drape, "With One Bet, Stablehand Becomes Stable Owner," *New York Times*, May 3, 2013, www.nytimes.com/2013/05/04/sports/conor-murphys-big-bet-bankrolls-horse-training-career.html?_r=0.

8. Blaise Pascal, *Pascal's Pensées* (New York: Dutton, 1958), 67.

9. Lydia Saad, "Three in Four in U.S. Still See the Bible as Word of God," June 4, 2014, Gallup, www.gallup.com/poll/170834/three-four-bible-word-god.aspx.

10. Jeremiah 29:12–14.

11. Deuteronomy 4:29.

12. Proverbs 8:17, NASB.

13. James 4:8, NASB.

14. Luke 19:10.

15. *Scarface,* directed by Brian De Palma (Universal Pictures, 1983).

16. Luke 15:11–12.

17. Luke 15:13.

18. *The Victoria Advocate,* June 20, 1997, Section C, 2.

19. Luke 15:13.

20. Luke 15:30.

21. Genesis 1:4, 10, 12, 18, 21, 25, 31.

22. Genesis 2:18.

23. 1 John 4:16.

24. 1 John 4:10.

25. Romans 5:5, NIV 1984.

26. *Marvin's Room,* directed by Jerry Zaks (Scott Rudin Productions, Tribeca Productions, and Marvin Productions, 1996).

27. Erwin Raphael McManus, *Soul Cravings: An Exploration of the Human Spirit* (Nashville: Thomas Nelson, 2008), Destiny, entry 1.

28. Jeremiah 1:5, MSG.

29. "Tom Brady Talks to Steve Kroft," *60 Minutes,* June, 2005. www.cbsnews.com/news/transcript-tom-brady-part-3/.

30. Pat Williams and Jim Denney, *What Are You Living For?* (Ventura, CA: Gospel Light, 2008), 51.

31. Ben Moshinsky, "Bank of America Intern's 5 A.M. E-Mail Before Death Worried Mom," Bloomberg, November 22, 2013, www.bloomberg.com/news/2013-11-22/bank-of-america-staff -quizzed-as-coroner-probes-intern-s-death.html.

32. Ephesians 2:10, NASB.

33. Frederick Buechner, *Wishful Thinking: A Theological ABC* (New York: Harper & Row, 1973), 95.

34. Luke 15:15–16.

35. Genesis 1:31.

36. *Bruce Almighty,* directed by Tom Shadyac (Spyglass Entertainment and Universal Pictures, 2003).

37. Job 38–41.

38. Romans 8:21.

39. Genesis 3:13.

40. Dietrich Bonhoeffer, *Letters and Papers from Prison* (Minneapolis, MN: Fortress, 2010), 479.

41. Luke 15:17.

42. John 10:10.

43. Psalm 103:11–12, NLT.

44. Steve Hartman, "Secret Santa Inspires Heroin Addict to Clean Up," CBS *Evening News,* December 16, 2011, cbsnews.com/news /secret-santa-inspires-heroin-addict-to-clean-up/.

45. Matthew 25:42–43.

46. Shane Claiborne, *The Irresistible Revolution: Living as an Ordinary Radical* (Grand Rapids, MI: Zondervan, 2006), 117.

47. John 11:25–26, NIV 1984.

48. Luke 15:17.

49. Luke 15:20.

50. Retold from Brennan Manning, *The Ragamuffin Gospel* (Sisters, OR: Multnomah, 2005), 127–34. Used with permission.

51. 2 Corinthians 7:10.

52. LifePlan, Paterson Center, www.patersoncenter.com/lifeplan /paterson-lifeplan.html.

53. See Luke 15:17–18.

54. Luke 15:18–20.

55. "Willard Words," DallasWillard.org, www.dwillard.org/resources /WillardWords.asp.

56. See Acts 3:19.

57. Retold from Philip Yancey, *What's So Amazing About Grace?* (Grand Rapids, MI: Zondervan, 1997), 49–51.

58. Luke 15:20.

59. Luke 15:20.

60. Luke 15:21.

61. Kurt Wagner, "Revisiting the Agony and Resilience of Redmond's Barcelona Race," *Sports Illustrated,* July 15, 2013, www.si.com /olympics/2012/07/13/derek-redmond-2012-london-olympics.

62. Josh McDowell, *More than a Carpenter* (Wheaton, IL: Tyndale, 1977).

63. Matthew 1:23.

64. Interfax–Religion, "Gagarin Never Said He Did Not See God in Space," April 12, 2006, www.interfax-religion.com/?act=news&div =1287.

65. C. S. Lewis, "The Seeing Eye," in *Christian Reflections* (Grand Rapids, MI: Eerdmans, 1967), 167–68.

66. Philippians 2:8.

67. Charles Dickens, *A Tale of Two Cities* (London: James Nisbet, 1902), 428.

68. Jeremiah 29:14.

69. 2 Peter 3:9, MSG.

70. John 14:6.

71. Matthew 4:19.

72. Matthew 10:32.

73. Quoted in Lee Strobel, *The Case for Faith: A Journalist Investigates the Toughest Objections for Christianity* (Grand Rapids, MI: Zondervan, 2000), 11.
74. Strobel, *The Case for Faith,* 17–18.
75. Augustine, *Confessions,* trans. R. S. Pine-Coffin (New York: Penguin, 1961), 21 (I,1).
76. Luke 15:21.
77. Luke 15:22.
78. Luke 15:23–24.
79. Vicki-Ann Downing, "Dick Hoyt, who runs marathons with his disabled son, impresses at Freshman Family Weekend," Providence College, November 17, 2013, www.providence.edu/news/headlines/Pages/Freshman-Family-Weekend-speaker-Dick-Hoyt-inspires-crowd.aspx.
80. "About Team Hoyt," Team Hoyt, www.teamhoyt.com/about-team-hoyt.html.
81. See Romans 8:1.
82. See Romans 8:39.
83. See Galatians 3:26.
84. See Ephesians 1:3.
85. See Ephesians 1:7.
86. See Ephesians 2:6.
87. See Ephesians 2:13.
88. See 1 Thessalonians 4:16.
89. Luke 15:6.
90. Luke 15:9.
91. Luke 15:23–24.
92. 2 Corinthians 5:17, NIrV.
93. Psalm 63:1–3, 6–8, NLT.

94. Psalm 63:2, NLT.

95. Psalm 63:6, NLT.

96. Greg L. Hawkins and Cally Parkinson, *Reveal: Where Are You?* (South Barrington, IL: Willow Creek Association, 2007).

97. 1 Samuel 3:10.

98. Cited in John Ortberg, *Everybody's Normal Till You Get to Know Them* (Grand Rapids, MI: Zondervan, 2009), 30.

99. Dallas Willard, *The Divine Conspiracy: Rediscovering Our Hidden Life in God* (New York: HarperCollins, 1998), 385–86.

100. "Expedia Trip A Day Giveaway—Find Your Spontaneity," www.youtube.com/watch?v=KI8LDZ9Kmgc.

101. Matthew 18:20.

102. John 3:16.

103. Matthew 16:25, NLT.

104. Genesis 12:2–3.

105. Mark Russell, *The Missional Entrepreneur: Principles and Practices for Business as Mission* (Birmingham, AL: New Hope Publishers, 2009), chapter 11.

106. Paul Tadalan, "Chalk the Block Chicago," www.youtube.com /watch?v=SMerVowcmVc.

107. Leonor Vivanco, "Mysterious Inspirational Chalk Messages Pop Up Around Chicago," *RedEye*, April 12, 2012, http://articles .redeyechicago.com/2012-04-12/news/31332529_1_chalk -messages-pop.

108. 2 Corinthians 5:17–19, NIrV.

109. Hebrews 13:5.

ABOUT THE AUTHORS

Dave Ferguson is founding and lead pastor of Chicago's Community Christian Church, a multisite missional community considered one of the most influential churches in America. Dave is also the visionary for NewThing, a global network of reproducing churches. Dave and his wife, Sue, have three children. **Jon Ferguson** is founding pastor of Community Christian Church, a teaching pastor for the church's Chicago network, and movement architect for NewThing. He and his wife, Lisa, have two children. Brothers Dave and Jon are the coauthors of three books on church leadership.

Take the Next Step

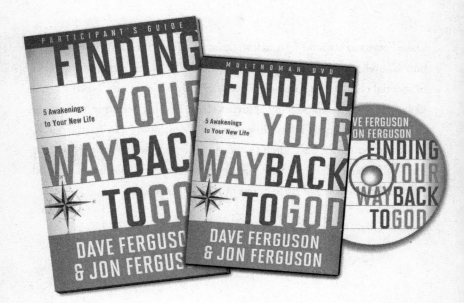

Perfect for individual or group study

The *Finding Your Way Back to God DVD* and the companion participant's guide explore the idea that we all want to find our way home—and back to God. In each ten-minute video on the five-part DVD, Dave Ferguson and Jon Ferguson guide you through life awakenings, inspiring you to follow the path God has laid out for returning to him. The participant's guide offers Bible investigation, life application questions, and prayer exercises to help you take positive action on your desire to find God.

Resources available | DaveFerguson.org | JonFerguson.org